Planning professional training days

Bob Gough and Dave James

Open University Press
Milton Keynes · Philadelphia

Open University Press
Celtic Court
22 Ballmoor
Buckingham MK18 1XW

and

1900 Frost Road, Suite 101
Bristol, PA 19007, USA

First published 1990

British Library Cataloguing in Publication Data

Gough, Bob
    Planning professional training days.
    1. England. Teachers. In-service training
    I. Title   II. James, Dave
    371.1460942

    ISBN 0-335-09412-0

Library of Congress Cataloging-in-Publication Data

Gough, Bob, 1931–
    Planning professional training days / Bob Gough & Dave James.
        p.   cm.
    Includes bibliographical references.
    ISBN 0-335-09412-0
    1. Teachers—In-service training—Great Britain—Planning.
I. James, Dave, 1943–   II Title.
LB1731.G64 1990
371.1'46—dc20   89-49165
                                                            CIP

Typeset by Colset Private Limited, Singapore
Printed and bound in Great Britain by Woolnough Bookbinding

Planning professional
training days

Baker days? Let's call them B-Days – everybody knows what they're for, but hardly anyone knows how to use them.

Ted Wragg

Contents

List of figures

Acknowledgements

We have very many people to thank, but in particular the teachers from the schools and the advisory teachers who worked with them on professional training days, for allowing us to use their experiences in the case studies.

This book is dedicated to the teachers of Britain, from whom we have learned so much, and who will take on – and succeed with – the challenge of training days, just as they have taken on all of the other challenges thrown at them.

Abbreviations

CIPFA	Chartered Institute of Public Finance Accountancy
DES	Department of Education and Science
DTI	Department of Trade and Industry
ESG	Educational Support Grants
FEU	Further Education Unit
GCSE	General Certificate of Secondary Education
GRIST	Grant Related In-Service Training
INSET	In-Service Education and Training
LEA	Local Education Authority
LEAP	Local Education Authorities Project (a management training project with LEAs and the BBC)
LEATGS	Local Education Authorities Training Grant Scheme
LMS	Local Management of Schools
PTD	Professional Training Day
SDP	School Development Plan
TGAT	Task Group on Assessment and Testing
TRIST	Technical and Vocational Education Initiative Related In-Service Training
TVEI	Technical and Vocational Education Initiative

Introduction

Over-worked teachers, under some strain, have not had many opportunities to learn about planning and organizing in-service education training (INSET) and, sometimes, not much time to attend any arranged by others. Consequently the quality of the experience of professional training days (PTDs) in schools has not always been as high as it might have been. This book aims to help those hard-pressed headteachers, deputy heads and other teachers who are given the task or arranging one or more of these days.

The first thing we have to say is 'Don't!', that is, don't just plan *one*. The resource that is now made available (albeit from taking teachers' holidays) will be much more valuable if it is planned coherently. All the professional training days should be planned together if possible, and – ideally – planned alongside all of the other INSET for teachers from the school. The starting-point for this planning should be the school development plan (SDP). All schools are required, under the regulations deriving from the Education Reform Act, 1988, to establish a national curriculum plan. Rather than be limited in this way, schools would be well advised (where they have not done so already) to formulate a total school development plan within which the national curriculum development plan would be embedded.

Staff development and INSET should derive from the SDP. The advantage of this is that the identification of INSET needs is no longer a one-off exercise, to be repeated every year (or whenever some money becomes available), but something that emerges from the SDP. Planning can thus be longer term and can be focused upon the real needs of the school and of the individuals within it.

The INSET process

In planning for professional training days, attention has to be given to the process as well as to the content, and this book will mainly be concerned with organizational arrangements, methods and styles. We are fairly sure that there will be no shortage of topics, themes and issues which schools might want to deal with, and some of these are predictable to some extent, in that the Department of Education and Science delineates National Priority Areas under the Local Education Authorities Training Grants Scheme (LEATGS) and also specifies certain key areas for consideration under the Educational Support Grant (ESG) scheme.

Eschewing the temptation to present a short, instant guide to INSET planning (even if it were possible, it would be something to avoid, in that many aspects of INSET require a reflective, measured approach), we shall, we hope, offer some suggestions which will be accessible to busy teachers in schools, enabling them to plan useful training days.

School improvement and staff development

INSET can be 'job-embedded' or 'job-related' (Nicholson *et al*. 1976): a PTD is clearly 'job-embedded'. While other types of INSET might, legitimately, have as their main concern the personal professional development of the teacher, the PTD is unambiguously and primarily concerned with school improvement. It seems fruitful to distinguish staff development from personal professional development, and Figure 1 is an attempt to do this.

Distinctions are made by a comparison between the intentions of the INSET, and the responsibilities of the provider, the employer and the teacher. On this analysis, a PTD is primarily a job-embedded, staff development enterprise.

Adult Education

INSET is, of course, adult education; some of the factors which make adult education effective are known to be:

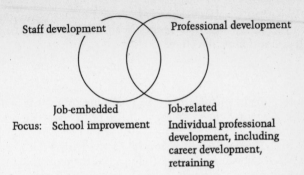

Staff development   Professional development

             Job-embedded   Job-related

Focus: School improvement   Individual professional
development, including
career development,
retraining

Figure 1   The relationship between staff development and professional development (from Gough 1985)

1   participant control
2   job-related tasks
3   provision of choice
4   opportunities to learn from one another.

Making arrangements for the provision of an in-service activity for a group of teachers certainly shares some of the characteristics of good lesson preparation:

1   Have ready all the resources you intend to use.
2   Be aware of the previous knowledge of the participants.
3   Know exactly how you will start proceedings.
4   Plan what the participants will be expected to do.
5   Ensure that the day starts and finishes on time.
6   Monitor the pace of activity: neither too fast nor too slow.
7   Aim to put the new knowledge or skills into a conceptual framework.

Two approaches to INSET

Herbert Altrichter (1986) points to two approaches to INSET: the teacher as a receiver of INSET, and the teacher as designer of her/his own INSET. We would argue that, particularly for PTDs, the latter approach should be predominant. When teachers are receivers, says Altrichter, INSET is seen as reception of knowledge in one situation, in order to apply it later in the classroom. Teachers are instructed by external agents who are thought to possess knowledge which is objectively valid and significant for teachers, independent of their specific working situation. This approach might be appropriate:

1   if INSET deals with comparatively simple or routine problems which are experienced by most of the participants in a similar way;
2   if INSET happens to fulfil several of the participants' specific needs and takes into account their prior knowledge;
3   if INSET does not purport to contribute directly to the improvement of classroom practice, but rather aims to provide teachers with a variety of interesting ideas, the application of which is left to the teachers.

The central problem of this approach is to bridge the gap between the information given and professional action, the latter depending on the experience of the participating teachers and the conditions for the implementation of the acquired knowledge. The teacher received too much and too little information at the same time because it is likely that the information is not perceived by him/her to be relevant to his specific situation and the problems which seem to be important to him/her.

Here a phenomenon can be observed which – in a medical analogy – is called 'tissue rejection' in organ transplants, because the supplied information may correspond neither to the previous experience of the teacher nor to the situations in which he has to act. The result is that it is difficult for the teacher to translate something from the program into his professional work.

(Posch 1985)

On the other hand, when teachers design their own INSET, it is seen as the development of the teachers' own knowledge and their professional situation by teachers themselves. Teachers who steer their own INSET are educating themselves by identifying problems relating to their professional life and by exploring them in order to clarify them and to develop new possibilities for solving them. Teachers are active in organizing their own professional learning; however, external agencies provide a supportive framework as a basis for the teachers' efforts.

Awareness raising

Everyone in education is conscious of the rapid pace of change: the nature of the changes has recently involved a quantum shift, with teachers (and headteachers) having to acquire new knowledge and skills. When the volume of change reaches the proportions it has today, it is a formidable task to keep up with it (sometimes it seems like quite an achievement to stand still!) Much recent INSET – focusing on the national curriculum or local management of schools, say – has been concerned with awareness raising. Many teachers are being left with their awareness highly elevated – and not much else. A Further Education Unit publication (FEU 1987) suggests a model, derived from Joyce and Showers (1981), showing several stages in the development of competence (see Fig. 2).

Needs analysis

Awareness having been raised, the next step is to define exactly what it is necessary to do. Many schools are now familiar with needs analysis methods, having engaged in TRIST (Technical and Vocational Education Initiative Related In-Service Training) and LEATGS procedures for several years. Needs will vary depending upon what has happened in the school already and the roles and statuses of those involved. An appropriate start is a clear identification and analysis of the present context.

Conceptual underpinning

We shall be continually suggesting that planning and delivery of INSET should be within coherent frameworks, and we in education should not be embarrassed about our need to engage in theory from time to time. 'Theory without practice is arid . . . practice without theory is blind.'

Skills development

Skills can rarely be developed by being talked at. One possible use of Figure 2 is to consider the different methods that might be used for the different stages. It may be possible to raise people's awareness by putting eighty of them in a room and talking to them; however, they will gain the skills of using computers only by practising on them, and will appreciate the relevance only by applying them in their own particular context. It may not be possible in the time

Figure 2 Stages in competence development

Roles	Awareness	Needs analysis	Conceptual underpinning	Skills development	Application on job	Evaluation
Headteachers						
Other senior managers						
Middle managers						
Staff development tutors						
Subject co-ordinators						
PBI						
Support staff						

available in a single PTD to give much opportunity for skills development, but if the PTD is planned as part of a total school approach to staff development, this should present little difficulty. If the PTD is a 'one-off', efforts would have to be made to provide such opportunities.

Application to practice

It is only when the knowledge and skills acquired during INSET are used in school settings that their relevance is made manifest. In some cases, they might need the support of colleagues, including headteachers. Co-operative planning of some piece of curriculum during a PTD and its application in the classroom is a good way of relating INSET to practice.

Monitoring and evaluation

This is dealt with in some detail in Chapter 5. As this model suggests, individuals with different roles in the educational enterprise may require different methods at different times and with different emphases.

1
Background and context

Teachers' Pay and Conditions Act, 1987

This Act brought to a close three years of teachers' 'working to contract'. There had also been various demonstrations and teacher morale was at a generally low ebb. Apart from removing teachers' rights to negotiation over pay, the legislation specified 'directed time', and increased the teachers' working year by five days when pupils were not present.

> a teacher employed full-time . . . shall be available for work for 195 days on which he may be required to teach pupils in addition to carrying out other duties; and those 195 days shall be specified by his employer or, if the employer so directs, by the headteacher.

(Some may be surprised by the implication that all teachers are male. Evidently equal opportunities perspectives have not yet reached the people who draft legislation.) Thus, every school in England and Wales has five 'professional training days' available. These are sometimes called (although not by us) 'Baker' days. Professor Ted Wragg, in the *Times Educational Supplement*, implied that abbreviation was permissible and labelled them 'B-days' on the grounds that everyone knows what they are, but no one knows how to use them.

We shall use the term 'professional training days' (PTD), since the more common 'Baker day' will become increasingly inappropriate (even if it ever were so), as the former Secretary of State for Education and Science pursues his political career elsewhere. The DES in various circulars use the term 'non contact days': although some of the time may be used for administrative matters, they are generally seen as in-service days. The Draft Circular (15 May 1989) on the Local Education Authority Training Grants Scheme (LEATGS) asks LEAs about the use of PTDs for training purposes. In order to provide some additional time for in-service education and training related to the introduction of the national curriculum, the secretary of state made two additional days available in the calendar year 1989 specifically for INSET purposes. In Circular 20/89 (18 August 1989) concerning LEATGS, LEAs are expected to use two or three of the PTDs in the Spring Term 1991 for the purpose of training for record-keeping and assessment for the 'basic curriculum and religious education'.

It is clear that PTDs constitute a major resource and are recognized as such by the DES in that they see them as a means of implementing change, as indicated by the specification of the timing and purpose of some of the days. The conduct of the days is the responsibility of the employer (the LEA). As the regulations from the Education Reform Act, 1988, come into effect, the implementation of the legislation (over a four-year period from April 1990) on local management of schools (LMS) will bring about changes: for some purposes, the governing body of a school will be the employer. It is clear, however, from the Interim Report of the Teachers' Pay and Conditions Committee, 1988, that the control of the PTDs will remain with the LEA. It is also clear from the DES Circular on LMS (DES 7/88) that specific grants, e.g. LEATGS, ESG, are exempted from the LMS provisions. This means that most INSET and hence PTDs remain a key responsibility of the LEA.

There has been a move towards an emphasis upon the school as the basic unit for INSET. The increase in school-based and school-focused INSET of recent years will be significantly reinforced by the onset of PTDs. There are dangers of an over-emphasis on school-based in-service education and training, because crucial aspects of INSET for the appropriate professional development of teachers may be neglected, or even ignored. A book on PTDs is not the place to develop this, since we are concerned solely with school-focused activity, except to say that teachers need (and deserve) a wide spectrum of education and training to fulfil their professional growth. Such a spectrum is likely to include provision from such sources as colleges/polytechnics/universities, as well as from the LEA (via teachers' centres, for example), the DES and various subject organizations.

One key change arising from this legislation is that – for the first time – all teachers are involved in INSET. Previously it had been possible 'not to opt in'. One consequence of this for PTDs is that the unit cost can be relatively low; it is not, however, cheap, since the teachers' time still has to be paid for, as well as the costs of materials and that of any external provider. It is worthwhile seeking to put a cost on a PTD, because those involved might think that the PTD comes for free. School-based and school-focused INSET should have an immediate relevance for the participants and be readily applied in the school: this is not always the case with other forms of INSET.

An integrated INSET policy

Professional training days are a part of a wider change. They need to relate to other INSET and staff development and are a means of involving all teachers in change. PTDs are under the control of the employer, unless the LEA chooses to delegate this power to the headteacher. Although there is a wide variety of practice, most LEAs retain control over some of the content and the dates for PTDs and delegate others to headteachers. When local management of schools is implemented the employer will become a mixture of the LEA and the governing body. DES circular 13/89 gives advice about employment responsibilities of LEAs and governing bodies, shows how the Education Reform Act has modified existing employment legislation and lists relevant legislation which is not changed by the Act and is relevant to schools. The overall position is unclear and it will take some time and, probably, a number of legal decisions before the position on employment of teachers is clarified.

The recommendations of the Interim Report of the Teachers' Pay and Conditions Committee (10 February 1989), in its section on LMS, advocates that almost all the LEAs' discretionary powers be passed to the governing body but specifically exempts INSET from those powers to be given to governors. In fact thirty-two powers are recommended to be given to the governing body and four are to remain with the LEA, with perhaps a fifth dependent upon current practice. One of the five powers recommended to remain with the LEA is control over professional training days.

Days of work [paragraph 36(i)(a)]. The LEA sets the dates of school terms at county, controlled and special agreement schools. It would seem logical that the LEA should also set the dates of teachers' work at county, controlled and special agreement schools; this logic is reinforced by the LEA's continuing responsibility for in-service training, for which some of the 5 days outside the pupil year of 190 days may well be used. (In voluntary aided schools the governors will continue to be responsible for setting the dates of teachers' work.)

This is in line with the exclusion from the LMS scheme of special grants which LEAs may not wholly devolve to schools. DES Circular 7/88 says that LEAs may continue the current practice of devolving INSET funds to schools, but makes it very clear that the LEA retains control over their use and that specific grants must be used for the purposes for which the grant was given and that LEAs retain the responsibility which cannot be devolved to schools. DES Circular 20/89 asks LEAs to say how within their overall INSET and staff development policy the different specific grants such as education support grant (ESG) and the technical and vocational education initiative (TVEI) relate to the Local Education Authorities Training Grant Scheme (LEATGS). In the questionnaire with this latest circular, LEAs are also asked how many of the professional training days are used for in-service education and training. In the questions on management of INSET the use of 'non-contact days' LEAs are asked to say if control of non-contact days are given to schools and if there are any arrangements for working at home on these days. Also in DES Circular 20/89 the use of some PTDs are specified for both content and timing:

> The Secretary of State expects authorities to set aside 2–3 non-contact days in the spring term of 1991 for this purpose.

This section is underlined and refers to those who will be involved in assessing pupils in the core subjects at key stage one in summer 1991. It seems clear that an integrated INSET policy is expected and that, within the INSET policy and plans, the professional training days are seen as a significant resource.

PTDs represent a major change. In-service education and training now includes all teachers, not just those who wish to become involved and are able to do so. INSET now has a high profile and is on every school's agenda as a daytime activity. The PTDs are also a significant INSET resource and represent one week of supply cover per year for every teacher. In a primary school with ten members of staff this is the equivalent of more than 0.25 of a full-time teacher and in a secondary school with forty staff it is more than the equivalent of a full-time member of staff. Teacher time on this scale is the most valuable INSET resource a school is likely to receive and it is the purpose of this book to help schools to use this valuable time to the best possible effect.

Emerging good practice

By the end of the academic year 1989/90 there will have been twelve PTDs: five for each year plus the additional two days granted by the secretary of state in recognition of the immense training needs for the implementation of the national curriculum. Good practice and interesting experiments in their use are already beginning to emerge.

Timing

The initial pattern was a day at the beginning of each term with another two chosen some time during the year. The use of PTDs at the beginning or end of half-term holidays obviously causes least disruption to pupils and their families and to teaching. PTDs at the very beginning of term are likely to be used for setting up for the new term rather then for INSET.

Using two or more days consecutively is another way to mini-mize disruption and the use of more substantial periods of time change the nature of the INSET which can be tackled and allows more in-depth work. The use of consecutive days does allow for more effective INSET.

Some schools have run staff conferences on Friday and Saturday or even on Saturday and Sunday, which can be a powerful way to run INSET, especially when the conferences are residential. An incentive for teachers is that by working at weekends they increase holiday time once more. The legal position is unclear but practice seems to show that while no one can be forced to work at week-ends, given agreement by the staff and the support of the governing body then using weekends is possible. The LEA controls days of work for county, controlled and special agreement schools and so could prevent weekend PTDs, but in voluntary schools the gover-nors control working days and so it may be easier for these schools to run PTDs at weekends and count the days towards the 195 working days.

Collaboration

Collaboration with another school is an increasingly popular way to use PTDs. Collaboration can lead to effective INSET as the very nature of joint planning encourages self-reflection. Collaboration between one or more schools over the use of two PTDs consecutively has been successful in sharing scarce resources of advisory teacher time or funds to buy in expertise. Schools who do this often work co-operatively on the first day and individually on the second day. Although there are additional costs of time and organization, such as attending planning meetings and negotiating the content of the day with others, the benefits of learning with others and of joint planning, implementation and review outweigh these costs.

Venue

The venue is an important consideration and can contribute to making the PTD a special event as well as reducing the possibility of distraction. Reasons for choosing a venue out of school have been to use specialist resources such as computer equipment, for improved facilities, to have pleasant surroundings, to be out of an LEA setting if issues of LEA control and hierarchy are relevant to the day, and to be on neutral territory when two schools are co-operating on some sensitive issue such as an amalgamation.

Non-teaching staff

Non-teaching staff are not automatically included in the professional training days. Where non-teaching staff are full-time appointments, their inclusion as appropriate presents no practical problem. However, the norm for part-time staff is for term-time work only; as the contracts for non-teaching staff have not been changed, it can be difficult to include non-teaching staff who work five days fewer a year than teaching staff. There will be occasions when the nature of the professional training day would not necessarily be enhanced by non-teaching staff being present but there will be many times when their presence will be important. For example, the Elton Report on behaviour will have an effect on school policy, practice and behaviour and it informs one of the national priority areas under LEATGS for 1990/91; similarly PTDs concerned with issues of school policy and practice for equality of opportunity would be relevant to all staff just as for an INSET day which focuses on school policy for discipline and behaviour. The role of the school secretary, caretaker, helpers and meals supervisors are important for any whole school policy.

Non-teaching staff could be paid to work additional days if the funds are available and if they chose to work the extra days. All of the non-teaching staff would have to agree to come for the day to be as successful as possible. It is possible that different days of work can be negotiated with non-teaching staff so that they could attend some PTDs as appropriate but then they would not be available at school on days when the pupils are present. Even when the presence of non-teaching staff is not required, to have some of them present can help the smooth running of the INSET day. The issue of non-teaching staff and their presence in school on professional training days is unclear and needs to be resolved.

PTDs and the development of INSET

INSET has always been an important part of education but during the 1980s there have been many changes of emphasis and policy. The pace and scale of the changes in education generally have increased dramatically to the point of current overload brought about by the Education Reform Act, 1988. This Act has introduced the most radical changes but is only the latest in a number of Education Acts in the 1980s. The list of current changes still working through the education system or about to enter it – special educational needs, GCSE, LMS, opting out of LEA control, national curriculum, parental choice, and so on – all have INSET implications. It is a very simplistic model for specific grants to be allocated for INSET to bring about these changes. Within the INSET resources available to schools PTDs are the major resource. The use of specific grants are not new: many local authorities have made them available for promotion of specific policies, for example some inner city Labour LEAs in promoting policies for equal opportunities and the Department of Trade and Industry (DTI) in making a number of specific grants available to schools to support the purchase of computer hardware and software. INSET has always been an important element of these specific grants: for the DTI scheme it was a requirement for staff to attend INSET courses on the introduction of computers into schools.

A major change came with the introduction of Grant Related

In-Service Training (GRIST) which followed the model set by the Technical and Vocational Educational Initiative (TVEI) and the training related to it, TVEI Related In-Service Training (TRIST). GRIST was renamed the Local Education Authorities Training Grant Scheme (LEATGS). The major changes for INSET as a result of GRIST/LEATGS were that every LEA is now expected by the DES to have an INSET policy and funds are allocated to all LEAs by the DES according to a formula based on the number of pupils and students in the LEA. The former position was much more variable, with some LEAs having INSET policies and allocating substantial resources to INSET while others did not. The old pooling arrangements whereby a large percentage of INSET expenditure, usually about 75 per cent, could be reclaimed from the DES via the pool were discontinued.

LEATGS

An indicative allocation for INSET was set for every LEA: this allocation is not an entitlement to grant but is an assessment by the DES (based upon the numbers in the pupil and student population) of the size of the INSET budget for every LEA. The indicative allocation is made up of two elements: national area priorities, which attract grant at the rate of 70 per cent (until 1990/91 when the rate of grant will be reduced to 65 per cent), and local area priorities, which attract grant at the rate of 50 per cent. LEAs are free to spend further money on INSET over the indicative allocation but the entire INSET policy for the LEA, including those elements for which there is no government grant, is subject to approval by the DES before any grant is payable. The emphasis is upon an integrated LEA INSET and staff development policy implemented by various government funds. The PTDs are a significant resource for LEAs and schools in implementing INSET policy.

The emphasis within GRIST and then LEATGS is on overall policies for INSET and consultation about INSET needs for the LEA, the school and individual teachers. This requirement for consultation has resulted in INSET needs identification procedures being set up within LEAs and within schools. The move towards school development planning and the new requirement for a national curriculum school development plan all give rise to INSET priorities being established by schools as a means for change and development. Within this context the INSET needs of individual teachers are now firmly set in the context of school, LEA or national priorities as these are the sources of funding. The capacity for INSET to support individual needs and interests has diminished. All teachers and all schools are now involved with INSET and the single most valuable resource is the five professional training days which are steadily being incorporated into INSET planning as a major means of bringing about change.

Summary

Professional training days are a significant resource, the use of which needs careful planning and integration into a wider staff development and in-service education framework. PTDs are an example of the change in education and INSET over the past few years. The school is now the basic unit for INSET and has the major responsibility for staff training, which must be an important part of school planning. INSET at school is relatively inexpensive and easy to run, yet has the attractions of relevance and immediate application, as working with fellow members of staff is more likely to result in changes in teaching and learning and in more support from colleagues. The active involvement and support of senior staff is crucial. Institutional needs are seen as being more important than those of individual teachers. Planning INSET need not be reduced to such a crude polarization and there are ways to protect the INSET needs of individuals within an overall school plan. This involves open management styles and consultation; planning over time and school development plans. INSET priorities and planned staff development will be derived from the consultation and the school development plan. The use of external INSET and advisers is important but should be part of a planned INSET programme for the school. The use of PTDs is likely to be the major resource for INSET; PTDs will be effective only if seen as part of school life and INSET priorities and plans.

2
Case studies

Planning the day

Preliminary arrangements

You have now decided the theme for the day; you have arranged for the external people to come at the appropriate time, and you have given them a clear and detailed briefing. (See Chapter 4 for guidelines on planning in detail.) You have gathered together the equipment and materials you will need for the day – video-recorders, projectors, paper, handouts, OHP transparencies, etc. – and you have determined the composition of any groups that will operate during the day, as well as identifying the purpose of each group activity, and the rationale for their establishment.

Timing

A timetable for the day should be prepared: every attempt should be made to adhere to the timings set, but they are NOT set in concrete. Keeping to the target times promotes effectiveness, but organizers should have enough flexibility to allow for dealing with unanticipated events (like a particular discussion taking longer than expected, but being too important to curtail).

Coffee/tea breaks should be included and, again, kept to time. (Usually it is better to resist the temptation to 'collect coffee and continue with the discussion over it'. A structured break not only gives people a chance to stretch (and to deal with necessary bodily functions) but also allows the mind to wander more freely and this often enables a freshness of approach when the group re-assembles.)

Lunch

Lunch should be as unlike a 'normal' lunch-time at school as possible. This could involve outside caterers, if funds are available. Efforts should be made to create a suitable atmosphere conducive to relaxation. The lunch break should be long enough to avoid feelings of haste to get it over, but not so long that the day loses some of its impetus. If viewing a videotape is part of the programme, it could be seen at either the beginning or the end of the lunch period. If used at the end, it signals the start of the afternoon session, in that it gently brings lunch to a close and focuses upon the next theme. If used at the beginning, it encourages the notion that (at least part of) the lunch-time can constitute a time resource.

Start the day right

It will usually be of benefit to start the day with an 'ice-breaker' (for examples, look at the Open University Pack P536 – Open University 1985) and the accompanying book by Patrick Eason (1985). Most people will know each other very well, of course (unless the PTD is for several schools) and so the activity should not be of the 'getting to know you' kind. It will, however, serve to give everyone the opportunity to

1 relax;
2 unpack some of the things which are in their mind (such issues as problems of traffic, which have made them start the day in a negative frame of mind, things which are going on in the school which are 'bugging' them, problems at home with the family: the point is not to bring out those problems, but to provide a framework such that they can be set on the back-burner for a while);
3 tune in to the focus for the day.

This should not be allowed to take up an undue amount of time, and the first session should *begin at the scheduled time*. Just as with teaching children, it is important to establish good habits: if PTDs normally do not get under way until 20 minutes or so after the scheduled starting time, then teachers will tend to arrive 10, 15 or 20 minutes late.

If you are having an 'outside speaker' (see pp. 48, 55), you need not always start the day that way. A group activity identifying some elements of the school's life and practices might well be a fruitful beginning.

Groups

If there are to be 'group activities', there should be clarification of the issues involved, e.g. What is the purpose? How will you start? Will there be group leaders? How will they be briefed? How long will you allow this to go on? How will you conclude it? How will an account be made? How (if at all) will it be 'reported back'? To whom? Why? (See also pp. 69–70.)

Structure

The operation of the day should be structured in terms of a model which should not only be related to that of other such days, but also be embedded in an over-arching plan for school and staff development. The model or framework that you use needs to be one with which you are comfortable and which is appropriate for the particular context in which you are working. The examples which we offer are not to be taken as recommendations, but – in talking through these – a headteacher, deputy head or staff development tutor might be helped towards an appropriate model.

Malcolm Skilbeck (1976) offers the model shown in Figure 3.

A simplified version of this has appeared in several texts related to staff development (see Figure 4).

A common approach, found in several sources, seems to be broadly similar:

1 Where are we now?
2 Where do we want to be?
3 What do we have to do to get there?
4 How do we know when we have done it?

The Schools Council Materials for Curriculum Planning Unit (Schools Council 1978) suggested that the responses to four key questions (and further questions derived from them) offer a framework for planning.

1 Why? (Why this topic? Why in this way? Why these people? Why now?)
2 What? (What is your starting-point? What has happened up to now? What is it that you want to achieve? Today? This term? Over a year?)

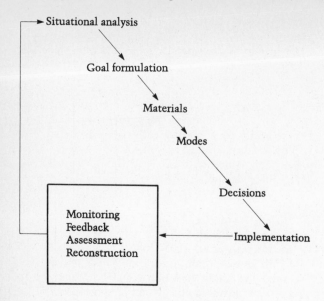

Figure 3 Model for a professional training day

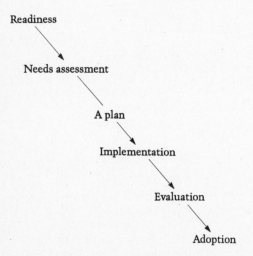

Figure 4 Simplified model for a professional training day

3 Who? (Who is to be involved? As participants? As 'presenters'? Why these?)
4 How? (How is it to be done? Which methods – and why? How will you know what has been achieved? See also Chapter 5.)

The case studies which follow are presented as examples – not necessarily of good practice in every case – to illustrate some of the issues about the planning and organization of the day. They are drawn from both primary and secondary schools.

Case study one: a common approach to the primary curriculum

Background

This was a joint PTD for an infants school (with nursery class) and a junior school on the same site. Both schools are large. The infants school has 270 children plus 50 nursery (part-time) children in 9 classes with 10 staff and is a group 4 school. The junior school has 325 pupils in 12 classes with 16 staff (including part-time teachers) and is a group 5 school.

Preliminary planning

Despite the growing and existing close co-operation between the schools a 'neutral' venue was thought to be very important, given the nature of the meeting. The local teachers' centre is not only neutral but also easily accessible and free. An excellent lunch was provided by the school catering service and the cost charged to the schools. The centre also set up AVA equipment and obtained the videotape required. The whole day was planned and organized by an advisory teacher.

Programme

9.00–9.05   *Introduction* (in seminar room): welcome and the programme for the day explained by the advisory teacher and the headteachers.
9.05–9.15   *Ice-breaking activity*: whole group. A 'pairing' activity when members of staff paired across the two schools and discussed existing contacts, hopes for the future and the programme for the day. Organized by the advisory teacher, a prompt start was made.

9.15–9.45	*Advisory teacher input* for the whole group: 'Continuity – implications and issues'. Continuity is a recurrent theme and part of the national and local primary inspectorate policy. The national curriculum and assessment emphasized to bring out the need for, and advantages to children and staff of, continuity and progression.
9.45–10.00	*Ice-breaking activity* (in seminar room): to write down ideas individually and then share in pairs what you think the issues and implications of the national curriculum are for you.
10.00–10.30	*Group activity* in small groups of four in different rooms in the centre (list given out).
15 mins	Each pair to share with each other what they felt the issues and implications were.
15 mins	As a group, agree two or three of the most important with reference to continuity.
10.30–10.45	*Coffee*: the centre has coffee/tea readily available and served.
10.45–11.00	*Whole group activity* (in seminar room): every group reports back on their two or three most important issues for continuity.
11.00–11.30	*Group activity* (eight people in three groups in different rooms in the centre): what strategies can we use to help our two schools work together effectively? This is the first time the flip-chart has appeared: at first a brainstorming exercise, but the task is to produce a brief list with comments. Advisory teacher explains the task.
11.30–11.45	*Whole group activity* (in seminar room): report back to one another their list. Advisory teacher draws out comparisons, stresses strategies and comments as to effectiveness.
11.45–12.00	*Review of the morning session*: in what ways have the morning's activities helped in thinking about and clarifying continuity?
12.00–12.30	*Whole group*: a pre-lunch drink and viewing of videotape on national curriculum (a pleasant, effective and different form of input). Comments on variety of activities and balance in the day.
12.30–1.30	*Lunch*: provided in the centre.
1.30–2.00	*Continuity windows*: the same groups of four as

	10.00–10.30 am in the same rooms. Review of issues concerning continuity, using feedback from other groups and input; advisory teacher sets and clarifies task.
2.00–2.30	*Whole group activity* (in seminar room): feedback with opportunity this time for clarification and discussion.
2.30–3.15	*Formulating an action plan.*
5 mins	Individual activity.
5 mins	Sharing in pairs.
20 mins	Producing plans in same small groups: which aspects of continuity can be worked on now? List: order them? What strategies can be used to begin and make progress? List: who will do what?
15 mins	Plenary session: groups report back and advisory teacher chairs, notes and produces a report for everyone.

Role of the advisory teacher

1 Planning: giving teachers confidence that they could do it and helping with detailed planning and roles on the day.
2 INSET: offering technical advice about managing INSET process.
3 Liaison: arranging with the centre to provide rooms, coffee, equipment, videotape, and so on.
4 Facilitator: enabling the two headteachers to take part by taking on the role of organizer on the day.
5 Pace: keeping the day going from one activity to another, getting the day to flow and making sure the groups were working as groups as well as being on task.
6 Plenary session: running this is a definite skill and also prevents headteachers taking over.

Commentary

This PTD was very well received by the teachers taking part; the evaluation built into the day – 'Formulating an action plan' – enabled participants to reflect upon what had been learnt and plan subsequent action. The day was heavily reliant on the involvement of the advisory teacher, who made all the preliminary arrangements and ran the day so that it flowed smoothly. The amount of work involved in planning, organizing and liaising both between the schools and with the centre was considerable. If the advisory teacher had not been able to do it, then either one teacher would have needed to devote a great deal of time, or the tasks would have had to have been shared between staff. The topic for the day was part of current thinking by both the schools and fitted into their overall INSET policy and school development plans.

The day was planned for a mixture of input, outside help and participation by the teachers and the involvement of those taking part accounted for the majority of the time. The day began and finished on time. Of the six and a quarter hours of the PTD, five hours were contact time with a fifteen-minute coffee break and an hour for lunch: both coffee and lunch were taken in the centre, and there was inevitably some further discussion of the content of the day during these periods. Teachers were actively involved – individually, in small groups, or as a large group – for three hours and fifty-five minutes. One hour and five minutes were spent on the talk given by the advisory teacher and on viewing the video-tape. The group activities were varied in format and in composition of the groups; they involved individual work, work in pairs and in groups of four and eight as well as the whole group together. The day was planned to have a variety of activities with a mixture of input and involvement and developed a momentum which showed the pace and variety had been planned well.

Case study two: TGAT, national curriculum and the Kingman Report

Background

This PTD was for a large primary school which has 430 pupils (with a nursery) with 19 staff (including part-time teachers) and is a group 6 school.

Preliminary planning

This programme was for half a day only, the other half being used for the traditional preparation activities for the first day of a new term. The session took place at school between 9.15 am and 12 pm and was organized by a primary advisory teacher who has an established working relationship with the school.

Programme

9.15–9.30	*Introduction*: looking at the language of the national curriculum and the TGAT report. This was done as a series of activities building up to a whole group view.
5 mins	*In pairs*: look at the statements and note those terms you are familiar with and those with which you are not.
5 mins	*Group activity* in groups of six (three pairs join): share and compare to build up a group view.
5 mins	*Whole group activity* (chaired by the advisory teacher): each group reports briefly on those terms known and unknown with comments from the advisory teacher and a handout given to define the terms.
9.30–9.50	*Advisory teacher input* for the whole group: brief lecture on TGAT, the national curriculum and concentrating on the English language part through emphasis on the Kingman Report. The advisory teacher aimed to give the overall context, pick up points not understood that arose from the first activity and then focus on language. The talk lasted for 15 minutes; questions were limited to points of fact and clarification. The talk was based on prepared overhead projector slides, copies of which were available as handouts.
9.50–10.30	*Group activity* in the same groups of six: this was carefully organized by the advisory teacher, who explained to the group as a whole. The task relied on the use of prepared sheets, the three core foundation subjects being given sheets of different colours. The task was to produce a list of what children would need to know for the profile components selected for the three subject areas and then to suggest some broad concepts and areas of knowledge which would encompass these items. The task was set in three parts:
15 mins	What do children need to know?
15 mins	Decide upon broad concepts and knowledge.
10 mins	Brief report back from the groups. The advisory teacher summarized using a flip-chart.
10.30–10.50	*Small group activity*: how can we make it happen?

Use the results of the previous discussion and the sheets of information displayed in the room to produce a list of strategies for action, to be written on flip-charts and pinned up.

10.50–11.00   *Coffee*.

11.00–11.30   *Whole group activity*: each group reports back their suggestions for practical action. The need for joint action, planning and implementation and assessment are stressed; any outstanding difficulties with the framework of the national curriculum are dealt with.

11.30–11.50   *A short talk*: the national curriculum – the timetable for implementation and assessment. The talk stresses the importance of retaining good primary practice and making the national curriculum fit within this, and the need for close collaboration between staff.

11.50–12.00   *Review*: what has been learned and what do we need to do next? All the teachers wrote down several answers to these questions and then points from individuals were recorded for use at a future staff meeting.

Commentary

This session was heavily reliant on the work of the advisory teacher, her knowledge of the school, her preparation of all the materials and her control of the session. This PTD could have been usefully extended to the afternoon session as there was a great deal of information and not enough time for teachers to begin to apply it to their own situation. The advisory teacher ensured the morning was a success by detailed planning and preparation. The day could have been run by staff in the school but perhaps not so intensively without a great deal of time and effort and, even then, members of staff would not have the advisory teacher's INSET experience and expertise in running such sessions.

Of the two and three-quarter hours timetabled for the PTD, ten minutes was allowed for coffee, twenty minutes were taken up by the short lecture by the advisory teacher and five minutes in explaining and clarifying tasks; the teachers were actively involved in a variety of different group work activities for the other two hours and ten minutes. Coffee actually took fifteen minutes and then it was difficult to get people back on task: domestic breaks have to be planned carefully and there is a temptation, especially with crowded programmes and little time, to try and get them over in an impractically short time.

The topic for discussion was highly relevant to the needs of the school and the teachers to begin the planning of the national curriculum and to understand the thinking behind the TGAT report. The group work was carefully structured in advance by the advisory teacher and the teacher with responsibility for language work. Evaluation was included in the twenty-minute session 'How can we make it happen?' and in the brief review at the end, which focused upon what had been learnt, what else needed to be done and action planning for the next meeting.

Evaluation

These two primary school case studies are examples of the involvement of advisory teachers who had the necessary INSET experience and skills to plan and run a PTD well. Working alongside outsiders with this expertise is one way for staff to learn the skills of planning, preparation and evaluation, although the time required to prepare overhead projector transparencies, produce handouts, preview videos and arrange the domestic details can be very difficult for hard-pressed primary teachers to find.

Case study three: staff appraisal

Background

The school is a boys' comprehensive in an inner-city area, the roll of which has declined substantially in recent years, and which consequently faces amalgamation within the next three or four years. The school has 450 pupils with 25 full-time members of staff and is a group 8 school. The LEA had made no plans at all and had not signalled to schools what might be in mind. There had been an informal working group of headteachers and others in senior positions in schools, meeting as a seminar at the teachers' centre for a couple of years. Some of the documents which this group has produced were used.

The headteacher and senior management team would like to get an appraisal system, acceptable to them and to the staff, in place before a perhaps inferior scheme is imposed.

Preliminary planning

The school has planned a series of PTDs, which are related not only to each other, but also to the themes being explored at staff and departmental meetings. Planning for this day – and other activities concerned with appraisal – is being done in co-operation with the local INSET co-ordinator, who will in fact make a contribution to the PTD.

Some time has been spent clarifying the school's policy on appraisal. The headteacher has made clear that the focus should be on *professional development*, the ultimate aim being 'the improvement of learning opportunities for all pupils'. The staff are aware, then, that judgement of teachers with a view to their reprimand or dismissal forms no part of the procedure. Attention of the staff has been drawn to the experience in Suffolk (Suffolk Education Department 1985; 1987) which had a pilot programme in teacher appraisal, from which some experience can be gained.

With the encouragement of the INSET co-ordinator, the senior management team of the school have recognized the need for clearly defined aims for the school to be identified as a prerequisite for an appraisal scheme, and have worked at this together with defining an unambiguous management structure. Every member of staff now has a clear (and in many cases up-dated) job description.

As an individual task prior to the day, all the teachers were asked to undertake a 'reflective self-evaluation', for which they were given guidance notes and the assurance that their self-evaluation would not be used as a basis for appraisal.

The PTD was held on a Friday, immediately preceding a half-term break, so that after a hard day the staff would have a long weekend.

Programme

9.00–9.30	*Arrival and coffee*: the staff assemble in the room where the plenary sessions are to be held. This has been arranged with chairs set on three sides of a rectangle, with OHP and television monitor on the fourth side.
9.30–9.40	*Introduction*: individual task. Write down (anonymously) the tasks you do that you would really like to be appraised rigorously and those which you would not.

9.40–10.20   *INSET co-ordinator input*: talk on staff appraisal – premises, purposes and process.

10.20–10.40   *Group task*: self-appraisal.

10.40–10.55   *Plenary session*: summary, and setting a group task.

10.55–11.15   *Coffee*.

11.15–11.30   *Group task*: what aspects of a teacher's classroom performance would you identify as appropriate for observation and appraisal?

11.30–11.50   *Plenary session*: summary of dimensions identified and consideration of US schedules.

11.50–12.30   *Videotapes* of classroom practice: analysis and discussion.

12.30–1.30   *Lunch*.

1.30–2.00   *Group activities*: what form should classroom observation take? Preparation, observation, de-briefing and interview.

2.00–2.30   *Videotapes*: examples from pilot areas of aspects of classroom observation.

2.30–2.45   *Whole group*: discussion and summary.

2.45–3.15   *Whole group*: identification of aspects of appraisal not yet addressed.

3.15–3.40   *Review*: implications of the day both for policy and for practice. What have we learned? What do we need to do next? Action plan. Evaluation.

Commentary

Coffee beforehand was a 'do-it-yourself' arrangement in the staffroom, the way a normal day at the school started. It might have been more fruitful to signal that this was a different kind of day, perhaps by using a different room or having special coffee. As it was, people drifted in from just before 9 am until ten minutes after the first session was scheduled to start.

The PTD didn't start on time. The deputy head (who was in charge of the arrangements) was talking to two members of staff and did not finish until after 9.30. He then spoke to the head-teacher, indicating that 'we would wait for a few minutes'. There is a range of practice on this issue: we would argue for a strict adherence to time, unless there are overwhelming reasons for not doing so (and waiting for people who are late is certainly not one). The introductory activity here served several purposes, all of them well. First, as an 'ice-breaker', it was something everybody could do quickly and without difficulty. Second, it focused attention upon the theme for the day. Third, it involved participation right from the start.

The talk by the INSET co-ordinator was well planned and well delivered, giving the factual background and offering evidence from the pilot areas with clarity, brevity, good humour and appropriate use of an overhead projector. There were also detailed handouts, which themselves constituted a useful resource. A talk *can* be useful if it is to the point, and not too lengthy. (See also the section of lectures, pp. 55–6.) This one also led directly into a group task, which was to give some consideration to self-appraisal.

The group task was quite well structured, because the leader for the session had been well briefed and there had been detailed and effective planning for it. Its starting-point was the individual task that the teachers had been asked to do prior to the day. They had been given a guidance schedule, and the groups were asked to comment on the usefulness of the schedule as well as that of the task itself. These discussions were very lively and positive. Several improvements to the schedule emerged as a result. (Incidentally it became more demanding for the teacher!)

These suggestions were quickly and efficiently summarized in the short plenary session, led by the deputy head. This was well planned and obviated the interminable 'reporting-back' that is so often a feature of plenary sessions. (Some suggestions regarding report-back sessions are given on pp. 49–70.) He also introduced the task for the groups after coffee, which meant that the teachers did not have to reconvene but could go into their group activity straight after coffee.

Twenty minutes had been set aside for coffee. The headteacher and another senior member of staff had meanwhile transformed the staffroom: they had purchased a supply of Danish pastries from a local delicatessen and had made several jugs of real coffee. All the staff commented upon the 'civilized' nature of this, and it was clearly worth the effort (see also p. 81.).

People went back to their groups on time. The task now was to list those aspects of a teacher's classroom performance which should be identified for observation and appraisal. Although there was much animated discussion and, eventually, a plethora of extremely valid suggestions, a great deal of time was spent in some groups debating whether such things were subject specific or not. It would have been better, perhaps, to have raised this as an issue with the whole staff and to have agreed, for example, that 'effective communication regarding content' would be a common aspect.

The points raised in discussion were quickly summarized and placed in predetermined (but not advertised) groupings (pp. 57–61 refer to ways of handling group work). These were similar to those used by a US system, samples of the schedules of which were available for consideration. These evoked considerable interest, although there was some doubt about their applicability in a British context. They were talked through, and some familiarity gained with the main features.

Two videotapes of British classroom practice were shown and the teachers asked to use the US material to formulate views about the teachers concerned. The videotapes were timed so as to allow only two or three minutes of general questions before it was time for the lunch break.

After lunch, groups of five – each chosen to represent different subject areas within it – worked through a given task: how would you structure the classroom observation aspect of appraisal in terms of preparation, observation, debriefing and interview/dialogue, and what training needs can you identify? It was felt desirable to bring together the issues from the groups, as a means of reinforcing some of the key elements in the procedures. The whole group then viewed videotapes from pilot appraisal areas, focusing on classroom observation. This placed the earlier discussions in the context of real classrooms, teachers and pupils.

The group discussion was a means of establishing a clear consensus about what forms of classroom observation would be both acceptable and useful. Obviously during the single day it was not possible to address in sufficient detail all elements of the appraisal process. It is evident that the interview constitutes an important component of appraisal, and that this aspect of appraisal should be reviewed in some way before the next PTD.

The review of the implications of the day was conducted by the headteacher, at his suggestion: he felt that it would be appropriate for him to 'pull the threads together'. It was not particularly successful, probably because he did not adhere to the prepared plan. Instead of a structured discussion leading to an agreed 'action plan' and a fairly rigorous evaluation, there was some desultory conversation about the day. The headteacher was obviously pleased with it and was impressed with what had been achieved by his colleagues. He gave due credit and praise for this but, in doing so, did not enable a sufficiently clear summary of the day's activities to emerge, still less allow for a plan of action to be determined. Although some of this ground could be retrieved within the school context, an opportunity was missed. Planning for the *end* of a PTD is no less important than planning for the beginning: there are times, perhaps, when authority figures should be encouraged to leave well alone!

Evaluation

A short questionnaire was circulated at the beginning of the final session and all the teachers completed it before they left. A week later (i.e. just after the half-term break) the local INSET co-ordinator met with the headteacher and deputy head. They went back to the initial planning documents in order to explore whether the original objectives had been achieved. Mainly, they had.

The headteacher had hoped that a complete and detailed appraisal system would emerge from the PTD, but he was very satisfied with the progress made and recognized that his optimism was somewhat unrealistic. The INSET co-ordinator took this opportunity to comment upon the headteacher's handling of the final session, being able to use some comments from the staff questionnaire, for example that they were anxious to consolidate the experience that they had had and looked for positive follow-up. The headteacher recognized that it would have been valuable to identify some particular follow-up tasks on the day. He was able – the day following this meeting – to raise the issue at a heads of departments' meeting. The heads of department agreed that they would meet in three weeks' time, all having prepared some appraisal instruments, based upon the PTD, with a view to having a consistent, if not common, approach throughout the school. All commented in detail upon the sessions during the day and identified areas for improvement under similar circumstances. The clear delineation of certain tasks to be done was seen as a very positive way to structure things.

The headteacher and deputy head now feel much more confident about planning other PTDs, and will be prepared to explore more imaginative methods than they might otherwise have used.

Case study four: record-keeping

Background

The school is a mixed voluntary aided school with 550 pupils in 26 classes with 34 staff and is a group 8 school. It was reorganized three years ago (in common with similar schools) into an 11–16 comprehensive, the post-16 students from all the schools being gathered into a sixth form college.

Preliminary planning

The PTD was planned and organized by one of the deputy heads, who has responsibility for in-service education within the school. Although there has been some attention given to school-focused INSET in recent years, the PTD was a 'one-off' session, unrelated to any other planned PTDs. Some preparatory work had been done with the staff, however, in the area of record-keeping, in that some heads of department had met with the deputy head, who had asked them to prepare an account of the way records were kept in their departments, indicating any strengths and weaknesses of which they were aware. They had met on subsequent occasions and were encouraged to reflect upon the kinds of records kept and their validity for various purposes. The material from this was to form the basis of the first session.

Programme

9.00–9.30	*Arrival and coffee*.
9.30–10.15	*Group activities*: the teachers are divided into cross-curricula groups, each having two people primed to give an account of the record-keeping processes in their departments. (They are strictly restricted to a five-minute outline, but do have examples to show.) The point is to try to relate the type of record-keeping to the subject and/or material concerned.
10.15–10.45	*Plenary session*: reports from the groups are shared with everyone. A constructive criticism of every mode of record-keeping is thus available.
10.45–11.15	*Coffee*.
11.15–12.00	*Talk by a visiting speaker*: he has had much experience in this area, having worked in national organizations concerned with testing, such as examining boards and the Schools Council. He is extremely knowledgeable about the subject and can cite practices in other schools, in other parts of the country and show illustrative material arising from research. His emphases – and most of the subsequent questions – were

	upon problems of record-keeping in mixed-ability groups.
12.00–12.45	*Group activities*: the teachers are divided into subject/faculty groups and are asked to examine their current practices in the light of the issues raised in the previous sessions.
12.45–1.45	*Lunch*.
1.45	*Afternoon activities*: this is a voluntary aided school and the afternoon is devoted to a consideration of the religious aspects of the school's life. A member of the Diocesan Board will address the teachers and indicate the particular expectations parents have of a school like this.

Commentary

The morning got off to a somewhat sluggish start. The teachers meandered in from about 9 am until 9.40, ten minutes after the scheduled starting time. Coffee was a 'do-it-yourself' operation in the staffroom, and there was much desultory conversation as colleagues drifted in in ones and twos. Although it was probably quite a good idea for the first activity to be one that got teachers to consider their existing practice, it was almost 10 am before they were installed in the correct rooms with their 'leaders' and focused on the task. The importance of a prompt start needs emphasizing, and it would have been useful to have involved everyone together in a 'beginning activity'. This could be quite short, but would serve to get everyone orientated towards the day and to clear away some of the day-to-day 'clutter' that occupies the minds of all of us first thing in the morning. It would also be much simpler to despatch them to the separate rooms for the group session.

The first group session went very well. The teachers who had been asked to 'lead' had approached the task seriously and had all given time and effort in an attempt to make a clear and coherent presentation. They had also been well briefed in that attention was devoted not so much towards the records themselves as towards the reasons behind a particular kind of record-keeping being used in certain circumstances. There was a genuine sharing of experience, with colleagues pointing to their own rationales and, in some circumstances, finding themselves questioning it. This was in a supportive atmosphere and there was very little in the way of overt 'defensiveness'. There is no doubt that this was in part due to the very good inter-colleague relationships which are present in the school (and they are there because they have been worked at), but this was reinforced by the preliminary planning.

The plenary session began to get a bit turgid. The first two groups gave an (oral) account of their discussion and while there was much of real value and significance, after this the reports began to be repetitive and the deputy head (responsible for running the day) began to get anxious over time: coffee was due, there were still several groups to report, the visiting speaker for the next session had arrived, we knew that he had to leave immediately after his talk, and therefore he should really start on time. Consequently, not only did the groups reporting later get short shrift in terms of time, but also there was not an opportunity to tease out some of the key issues which had in fact been identified during the group sessions. A different mode of 'reporting back' (see pp. 69–70) would certainly have been beneficial here.

The coffee break was rather chaotic and again a 'do-it-yourself' affair: hardly conducive to a continued and measured discussion of the morning's sessions. The deputy head managed to use a combination of status and charisma to ensure that the visiting speaker was able to drink a cup of coffee in relative comfort. It really is worth the effort to try to do something special on these occasions.

The talk was excellent. The speaker knew his stuff, he had been well briefed, he kept to the point – and to time – and dealt with questions with great effectiveness and courtesy. There is nothing wrong with having outside speakers if they are of high quality and deal with the issues concerned in a manner that addresses the staff's needs.

The groups for the next session were determined either by departments where these were large enough to generate a usefully sized group, or in quasi-faculties of subject groupings just for this occasion. There was an airing of similarities and differences, which was quite stimulating, but an initial reluctance to take on board some of the messages from the morning. This stemmed from the realization that there was a lot of hard and challenging work involved. What would have helped here was a recognition on the part of the senior management team of the school of these implications and a commitment from them to identify resources – in terms of time, funds and people – to address them.

Lunch was quite well done and provided by the Home Economics Department at less than cost; it included a glass of wine courtesy of the unofficial staff fund, to which the headteacher gave a substantial donation from some other (non-LEA!) source to which he has access.

The afternoon session, devoted to diocesan matters, was not observed.

Evaluation

There was no structured evaluation planned or carried out. Some of the description above (via non-participant observation) obviously constitutes an evaluation, and this was made available to the deputy head. The afternoon session was not observed at the request of the deputy head, who was concerned that the representative from the Diocesan Board might have negative views about being observed. There was little purpose in challenging this sensitivity, since it was more important to preserve good relationships with the school. It was a pity, though, since the session was of particular relevance to this type of school, and it was a valid use of professional training time.

During the day, there was no overt decision to carry out any kind of 'follow-up', although clearly there were possibilities that presented themselves. This shortcoming and the absence of any action plans were pointed out to the deputy head together with a written account of the day. This PTD was very much a 'one-off' event and, although obviously valuable in many ways, it might have gained by being planned and organized within a wider staff development framework.

3
Methods and techniques

Introduction

There is no one best method for INSET: the task is to select methods and techniques in combinations appropriate to the purpose of INSET and the nature of the group. INSET should allow for the knowledge and experience of those teachers involved. Although participants in INSET are experienced teachers, they are not necessarily experienced at the topic of the INSET and may not be able to participate fully in all sessions. The many changes currently taking place in education will occasionally require straight-forward traditional input of information and learning of skills before teachers can apply their experience. The emphasis should remain on the practical and the relevant, however, which will be the case only if teachers contribute and share ideas and experience and plan for change together. Activities should be planned with a balance between the different methods and techniques to give variety and pace to the PTD. This chapter gives a wide range of INSET methods and techniques with a description of the activity and an example of its use, and comments on the advantages and disadvantages of each method. This list may be used to select appropriate methods for planning and running a PTD, but only a teacher with the knowledge of a school and those who work in it will be able to identify those best suited to a particular purpose. A summary of INSET methods and techniques for planning on pp. 71–85 may be photocopied for your personal use.

Conferences

Conferences are usually for relatively large groups and when well run and organized generate a momentum of their own. Conferences normally take place outside the participants' school and generally last for at least a whole day, using staff external to the school. Venue is important and may confer status on the activity. The use of hotels, conference centres and higher education institutions is increasing and, although expensive, this type of venue does create a sense of status which can add greatly to the effectiveness of the conference (provided that the rest of the arrangements work smoothly). Conferences are costly in both time and money and must be used effectively. Weekend conferences rely upon those present giving up their weekends and the domestic circumstances of some teachers may prevent their participation. The change of surroundings is important: residential conferences are a very powerful way to generate a group atmosphere and commitment to an idea or a change. Conferences are useful as the start of an INSET programme or the focus of a particularly significant stage in the development of a piece of INSET, but are rarely the conclusion of a series of INSET activities. Examples are the use of a residential conference by the staff of two schools which are amalgamating to give the teachers time to thrash out common philosophies and goals and to get to know one another, or using a day conference for a group of schools meeting to review a particular aspect of teaching and learning and then following up the conference in their own schools. Conferences are also used to launch major initiatives and can confer a high profile on the subject in focus. Conferences must be evaluated and followed up.

Visits and observation

Visits to other schools

Visits to other schools are a very popular method of INSET with teachers. To visit in school time is ideal but raises the problem of release and cover for the classes of the teacher making the visit. Visits involve observation of teaching and enable teachers to measure themselves in comparison with the teachers they observe. There is a general misconception that visits must be made to schools of excellence and that ideas can be taken and used immediately in the visitor's own school. Certainly visits should be made to schools to observe good practice but the perfect school probably does not exist and even if it did it would be impossible to replicate it quickly in a different situation.

Visits to nearby schools can be made for the morning session and the afternoon session can be used for debriefing. This form of visiting often works well within schools who are grouped together and work together on a regular basis, although the geographical locations are of course important to make the organization practical. Groups of primary schools, groups of primary and special schools, and groups of secondary schools and their feeder primary schools are all examples of suitable clusters.

If visits are organized to take place on a PTD, this should include the whole staff in primary schools so that everyone has a chance to participate in the follow-up, but in secondary schools internal visits can be organized on departmental or faculty basis to keep the organization manageable and provide a departmental focus within a whole school INSET plan. Other ways to organize visits for a PTD are to arrange a series of visits for different members of staff, so that not everyone is out at the same time: this requires an overall plan so that visits are incorporated and the results collated. Using the whole day allows visits to be made much further afield.

Visits and observations are very powerful INSET methods as they are to do with classroom interaction, the very heart of teaching and learning. Properly prepared they are useful and relevant. The data collected will provide insights into teachers' work. Reports on visits should be written up as they will form the basis for review; if visits are organized over a period of time, written reports will be needed for sharing the experiences with colleagues.

Preparing visits

It is essential that visits are well prepared and followed up. Unless this happens visitors only gain a general impression, pick up one or two tips and have little to contribute to colleagues as a result. A well-prepared visit can also be used as a part of INSET with colleagues. To over-prepare is also a danger: the visitor with detailed questionnaires is likely to upset the receiving teacher and find little more than the answers to the prepared questions. Some schools try to send two teachers to the same school at different times so that a pair of teachers can cross-check their experiences and prepare a report for colleagues. Given limited time and the problems of cover some schools deliberately visit as wide a range of schools as possible. The purpose of the visit will determine the strategy. The more specific the reason for the visit, the more likely it is that the purpose will be best served by concentrating visits to a few schools and more than one teacher making the visit.

Examples

A school about to purchase additional computers and thinking about school policy and classroom organization will send visitors to a wide range of schools and ask questions about security, access, organization of software, school policy and classroom organization to compile a lot of information before taking any decisions. Another school wishing to concentrate upon the use of computers to support language teaching will probably visit fewer schools but spend more time in particular classrooms, observe pupils working with language programs and discuss their use with teachers in the receiving school before making changes and purchasing additional software.

The receiving teacher

The receiving teacher should be briefed in advance about the purpose of the visit and be available to discuss the observation afterwards with the visitor. The presence of the visitor will change the classroom situation being observed. Aids to visits can be tape-recording or even video-recording of lessons, detailed schedules with specific points to observe or a specific aspect to focus on such as teacher and pupil talk, the extent to which the teacher dominates the talk, the attention given to boys instead of girls or time sampling of specific classroom events. These are all research-type methods which have their place but should be used only with the express permission of the teacher being observed and according to the contract negotiated between the observer and the observed. The receiving teacher should be given some feedback as a result of the visit. Other methods of observing in schools include shadowing a particular pupil to observe the experience from a particular pupil perspective, shadowing a particular member of staff, and exchanging roles with a member of staff.

Visits in own school

A visit within one's own school is a perfectly valid use of INSET time, if there is prior negotiation as to the purpose of the visit and debriefing afterwards. The potentially threatening nature of these visits can be diffused by careful preparation and the negotiation of a contract between observer and observed, with control over the results being kept by the receiving teacher so that anything revealed to colleagues is done only with the permission of the teacher observed. Making the visits reciprocal will reduce the potential threat, for example jointly planning a piece of work, observing or even teaching together, and then giving feedback afterwards. A popular way for such in-school visits to take place in the primary school is for the lead teacher for a particular subject to observe and work with colleagues. In secondary schools it will take place within a department or, more often with the increase of small departments, within a faculty. A particular example is a new teacher being observed and then observing an experienced colleague. Visits within the school have the obvious advantage of taking less time, being easier to organize and being cheaper as no travelling time or expenses are involved.

Visits out of school time

Visits out of school time are also useful, even without observation of teaching and learning, as a lot can be learned about the way the school is run, the organization of classrooms, the use of specialist equipment and materials, the use of learning resources and the quality and content of pupils' work through displays around the school. Access to another school's documents such as policies, planning and record-keeping systems, and reports and publications for parents and governors can also be very useful. Obviously the purpose of the visit will decide if an after-school visit is appropriate.

Meetings

Meetings can be an INSET activity or part of one, especially where some decision must be taken or a consensus reached, or for problem-solving. Certainly meetings are an important part of planning and evaluating INSET. There is a great deal of literature and INSET material on effective meetings: they must be well organized and run, with a definite purpose, be briefly and accurately recorded so that decisions are agreed and action taken, with a clear statement of who agreed to take what action and by what date. Meetings can be run by a team of people with a chair, a note-taker and a timekeeper. It is beneficial to record the main points on a flip-chart: not only can everyone see the main points but also the chair can point out time-consuming repetitions. The timekeeper is an important part of the team who can remind the chair that only a certain amount of time is left for an item; timely interventions can help the chair prevent one person's dominating the meeting or getting away from the point. The purpose of the meeting must be clear; notes of the previous meeting and agendas should be circulated in advance. Meetings are a part of the formal life of the school and INSET meetings help to integrate INSET into that life. Meetings which only give information are normally an inefficient use of time as the information could probably have been given in another less time-consuming manner. Meetings should not be too large for decisions to be taken. For proper participation, meetings should be no larger than fifteen people and for discussion to take place they should have no fewer than six people. With larger groups of people for substantial parts of the meeting the groups should be divided into smaller groups and the results of discussion subsequently shared with the whole group. The videotapes, *Meetings, Bloody Meetings* (1981) and *More Bloody Meetings* (1984) from Video Arts, both star John Cleese and are popular training material for running effective meetings. The Industrial Society produce a series of booklets useful for school management, including one on running meetings (Industrial Society 1982).

Learning resources

The review, selection and testing of new learning materials is a very good INSET technique. Teachers find examination of learning materials relevant to their work, for example the review of resources for racial or sexual bias. This is a very good way into sensitive issues as the content can be examined and the authors of the materials can be criticized before the manner in which the materials are used is discussed and criteria established for the purchase or development of new teaching materials to replace the discarded ones. A popular technique is to give teachers a small amount of money and ask them to purchase new resources. The criteria for selection can be agreed before or be left until after purchase, although in this case the amount of money for materials should be very small. Once the materials are brought back to school, they form the basis of INSET sessions with teachers explaining the reasons for their choices, how they have used them in the classroom and the reaction of the pupils. This is highly relevant to teaching and can lead to a discussion of teaching and learning. The analysis of children's work arising from the use of particular learning resources is another appropriate and productive method of INSET.

Lectures

This traditional form of INSET activity is no longer fashionable but still has its place. Lectures for any length of time are inefficient unless the speaker is very good, well prepared and able to entertain a large audience so as to retain attention. The use of devices to aid interest and concentration can also help the lecture to have an impact. The use of video clips, slides, overhead projection transparencies, audio tape and audience participation are all ways to enhance the traditional lecture. The use of an eminent person simply because of their status is unlikely to have any great effect on the audience. To invite the local inspector or adviser simply because they are the local inspector or adviser is not enough. The use of the lecture to a large audience can be a very cheap and efficient way to get a particular message to a group of people, assuming the lecturer is skilful; if the lecturer has high status this can be a way to indicate the importance of the INSET activity.

The lecture should be used sparingly, but it can be a good way to introduce a topic, provide specific information, arouse interest, raise awareness, generate enthusiasm, present a particular set of ideas or theory and occasionally inspire a group of people (see 'Awareness raising' on p. 17). The lecture can rarely be a self-contained INSET activity and almost always has to be followed up with some form of participation by the audience to apply the knowledge or ideas to their own situation. Lecturers on their own seldom change attitudes or behaviour and teachers must have an opportunity to reflect, consider the content of the lecture and think about any new skills for teaching and learning. The use of the lecture is still a popular form of INSET and is often the starting-point: when planning INSET beware of the traditional beginning of input from an expert. A good lecture from an appropriate person who has been well briefed and with the lecture planned into the INSET for a specific purpose can be very valuable, but lectures do need to be chaired, with speakers being introduced and very importantly any question-and-answer session after the lecture must be well chaired. With a large audience it is impossible to have a general discussion. Question time should be clearly agreed in advance and the chair should limit questions to points of information and fact only and deal ruthlessly with individuals who wish to make their points and raise issues. Questions should be repeated and if necessary summarized so that everyone in the audience knows what question was asked.

'Lecturettes'

The use of lecturettes is a good INSET method during a day's INSET. Short sharp lectures of ten to fifteen minutes can bring variety to a day, introduce information, refine thinking, present tasks for groups of teachers and make the INSET day flow. Where someone has taken control of a PTD, is well prepared and planned, and has a variety of tasks for the participants, the use of brief lectures with material prepared in advance but selected according to the reactions and stage of development of the participants can be highly effective. This orchestration of an INSET day using lecturettes within an overall framework to add variety is often used by freelance consultants and consultants from higher education.

Workshops

'Workshop' is an overworked term and ill defined. Workshops were a reaction to the traditional lecture and were used to describe any INSET activity that was not a lecture. At another level the workshop is associated with practical activities and usually the making of some product – either some teaching materials or trying out teaching materials for subsequent use. Workshops encourage participation by teachers and usually demand it. Workshops also use the experience of those involved so they can contribute to the session. Workshops must be planned and structured and have a clearly stated outcome or product, yet the plan must allow for modifications as the workshop progresses, otherwise it will not be able to accommodate the needs and experience of the participants. When the structure is too rigid and the activities too directed the value of participation may be lost. Workshops encourage sharing of ideas and experience and value what the members bring to the session. Workshops must be planned and led; the leader must be able to vary the detailed plan according to the participants' reactions. There should normally be an end product but this need not be a set of learning materials or a model or a piece of apparatus. The product could be a set of ideas or the first draft of a policy; the key elements are participation, involvement and the use of the experience of those taking part. Workshops can be threatening to individuals and so the ground rules and the tasks must be clear from the start, even with a group of teachers from the same school who have worked together for some time. Participants must know what is expected, how they can contribute and what will happen to the product. Workshops will be successful only if participants are confident, feel secure and are able to relax and contribute to the session.

Workshops can be expensive in terms of planning and preparation time, and when materials and equipment are needed for practical work. Participation requires relatively small groups of between six and fifteen; if a larger group divides to engage in workshop activity then there is even more planning and organization to do, as a series of workshops will have to run and decisions made about groupings and sharing of the results. Given the relative expense and the practical nature of workshops, substantial amounts of time should be devoted to them during a professional training day to give them the opportunity to be effective.

Group work

Group work is another ill-defined and over-worked INSET term which now regularly appears on INSET programmes and plans for PTDs. The emphasis of group work is participation, the use of the experience and skills of the participants, and their engagement and involvement in a task, problem-solving and planning for subsequent action, all very similar to workshops: in fact a workshop is a particular form of group work. The term 'group work' has taken over the general small group discussion meaning from workshop, which is now associated with some practical activity rather than just discussion. The emphasis on group work within INSET is fine, but unless it is carefully planned and structured with specific achievable outcomes in mind group work will become boring and be seen as a waste of time by those involved. 'Oh no, not another sharing of ignorance on a flip-chart' was the comment of teachers asked to join in group work which was not clearly planned and structured. Within group work there are many methods and techniques which can be used in a professional training day. The more carefully planned and structured the group work and the task, the better will be the experience for the participants. The size of the group, the membership of the group, leadership and nature of the task are all crucial elements in the planning for successful group work.

Brainstorming

Brainstorming can be a very quick and simple way to generate ideas and tap the experience of a group. The most usual method is for a small group of four to eight to record ideas on a flip-chart for presentation to the whole group at a later state. At best this can be a productive process but at worst a boring and repetitive exercise. Rules for brainstorming are that all ideas are accepted and recorded, the time available must be known, the group must be led, the use of the results must be known in advance and the task must be clear and acceptable to those taking part. Unless these rules are followed, brainstorming can become an exercise to please the organizer with those taking part agreeing to play the game but little else. Brainstorming can apparently produce results quickly but these will often be superficial. What is done with the results is the crucial question. If the results of brainstorming sessions are summarized on a flip-chart for all to see and the ideas categorized and subsequently used to solve a problem, take a decision, make the next step clear, produce a consensus or an agreement, then it is a useful technique. Beware of brainstorming sessions that result in many sheets of a flip-chart that appear to have no purpose, are never referred to again and of vague promises to write up the results and distribute them later. The purpose of the brainstorming session and the use of the ideas generated are the crucial issues.

Structuring group work

There are many ways to structure the work. Individuals can be asked to write down ideas on pieces of card or strips of paper. This ensures that everyone takes part and with good and sensitive leadership individuals can be asked to contribute their ideas. Individual statements can be pinned up on a display board or laid out on a table or the floor to build up an overall picture of the ideas from the group. Individuals could be asked to explain or elaborate and can be questioned by colleagues. The leader may join in but must ensure the rules agreed in advance are operated, that the timetable is met, and that individual participants are protected or drawn out as necessary. The ideas recorded on pieces of card can be pooled within a group by slowly building up a group list. Pairs can share the ideas written on their cards: the rules for this exercise are that each listens to the other in turn so that the ideas are explained, only then are questions asked to clarify the ideas and the ideas compared to produce a new refined list from the pair. This process can be repeated with pairs joining to form fours, and fours forming to make groups of eight, the maximum for this type of activity. How the information and ideas are to be recorded and presented to a larger group can be decided by the group but it should *not* be in the form of a long rapidly written list on a flip-chart.

Sharing the results

Sharing ideas as the result of brainstorming often results in a long list on several sheets of a flip-chart; at worst the ideas mean very little to anyone other than the person who recorded them, and at best they are meaningful only to the group who compiled the list. A summary of the first list is necessary for presentation to a larger group. The summary should be on one or two large sheets and not just in a long list with no particular order. Presentation of ideas in the form of a chart, a diagram or a grid will help the group when refining the ideas, explaining them to others, and writing up the results of the group work.

Cards: the diamond nine

Groups can be asked to place ideas on cards in an order of priority which focuses the discussion. This can be a very difficult task which is often made easier by the use of the 'diamond nine': the task is to determine an order of priority by placing the cards in a diamond shape, using nine cards with one top priority, two equal second priorities, three equal third priorities, two equal fourth priorities and finally this one at the bottom of the diamond (see Figure 5). This device is, of course, artificial but it does structure the session.

Cards: sharing ideas

Cards can be shuffled and dealt out, which gives access to the ideas of others in the group; this method ensures that discussion involves all members of a group and that the same people do not always work with each other. An alternative is to draw out cards in a 'lucky dip'.

Another way to structure discussion is to have a task of matching definitions to statements. This is particularly good for coming to

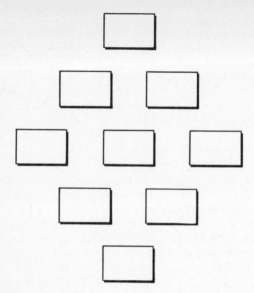

Figure 5   The 'diamond nine'

grips with new information as a task following an input such as a lecture, reading or watching a videotape. It is also a good way for individuals or a small group to find out what they already know and where the gaps in their knowledge are.

Cards: categorizing ideas

To structure a discussion, group members can be asked to write down their ideas on a topic or problem; a list can be built up by progressively increasing the discussion and the ideas refined by gradually increasing the size of the group, until the task demands that the ideas are grouped in some way for presentation to others. The headings can be set out on a large sheet of paper and participants asked to place their consensus statements on the cards in columns under the various headings. This task can be further refined by asking group members to agree an order of priority, perhaps by using a 'diamond nine'. In the discussion after the comparison and summary at the end participants can be told why the headings themselves were chosen and be invited to challenge them and modify the headings. Groups can also be asked to categorize their own statements and invent their own headings according to a set of explicit criteria. If enough time is available this method is preferable to giving predetermined headings as the organizer's ideas will not then influence the results as much. Plenty of time must be allowed for discussion and the problem must be explicitly stated, otherwise there will be no conclusions from the groups, who are likely to become either frustrated or dominated by powerful individuals.

Case studies

Real situations

Case studies provide good material for group discussion. If real cases are used, confidentiality is essential. Case studies based on a particular school are potentially very powerful but must be used with great care as everyone will know the situation and will bring personal feelings to the case study. Individual teachers and pupils must be protected and agreement from teachers, parents and pupils must be obtained, with a clear statement and guarantee as to the use of the material. A genuine case study for the school with appropriate documentation is a very useful and highly relevant way to involve teachers in a problem-solving activity for the benefit of the institution. The choice of the case and the way it is introduced and handled is crucial, as whole staff agreement on the next steps are essential. To use a professional training day for problem-solving using a particular case must not result in division amongst staff or the isolation of a small disaffected minority. The real case study approach is potentially rewarding but can be highly dangerous to the institution unless the case is carefully chosen and the rules agreed in advance and individuals protected as necessary. The discussion of the work or behaviour or particular pupils is a good example of a case study approach but the danger is that the discussion focuses only on the pupils and the particular problems involved; if case study material is used it should be linked to overall issues and principles and should not remain at the level of a specific case.

Amalgams

Case studies can be made up by amalgamating a number of real situations together. This can be a time-consuming process but the case study can then be made realistic and relevant to the particular school and the topic for the professional training day. The same conditions still apply: individuals and schools within the case study must be anonymous and permission must be given for materials to be used. To make up case study material is a very demanding and time-consuming task and one not to be undertaken lightly.

Commercial or fictitious case studies

The use of commercially produced case studies is far easier to arrange and use for INSET. The use of these INSET materials will be subject to copyright and the cost may be high; they also run the risk of being too general or not relevant to the particular school or issue under discussion. Obviously the selection of the case study material needs great care, otherwise the participants will interact with extraneous issues such as the differences between their own school situation and the ones represented in the case study. This can be a useful and legitimate activity, but only if the session is organized so that teachers engage with the issues of the case study as well. The Open University has a wealth of case study material as part of their many courses in the form of videotape and written material. The use of case study material from outside the school is a good way to approach potentially difficult issues by distancing those involved from their own situation, although the potential for irrelevance to the existing situation is, of course, increased.

Role play

Role play can be a powerful INSET technique but it is also potentially threatening to participants: there are likely to be some members of the group who will be reluctant to join in. Role play has to be extensively prepared and very sensitively and carefully led. The purpose of the role play has to be made explicit and the outcomes have to be relevant to the task under discussion. Even with a well-established staff who know one another well and have worked together for some time, role play can be difficult to set up and make productive. Participants must feel secure, must be able to contribute to the level at which they feel comfortable, and the rules of acceptability of individual contributions has to be made clear. Role play will not work unless such ground rules are clearly stated and agreed. Role play must have a firm basis in a realistic and well-researched situation so that participants have sufficient documentation and information about their particular roles. Structuring role play is a very time-consuming process and preparation must be thorough.

Some role play can be set up quite quickly and teachers asked to take part, but these sessions – while they can be enjoyable for some participants – rarely lead to anything other than an ice-breaking activity for a group. Role play can be a way of changing attitudes and subsequent practice. It is, however, a difficult INSET method to do well; it not only requires skill and experience but also is likely to be expensive in time and money to set up and run effectively. It is not an INSET method to be undertaken lightly.

Mini case studies

Mini case studies or situations are a very good way to use role play as the expense of time and money is likely to be less than a major case study or role play.

Triads

Triads are small groups of three working on a particular situation with a pair having roles in relation to a particular situation and the third person acting as observer. The situation can be a prepared one or a detailed issue can be given with participants filling in the details from their own experience. It is usual for all the people in the triad to exchange roles, having turns at being the observer and being observed in the two other roles of the situation. Rules for the group work in this form need to be made explicit. Issues of confidentiality are particularly important, especially if the participants are filling in details of particular issues from their own experience. There should also be guidance for the role of observer with emphasis on the recording of facts, of what was said and the manner in which participants reacted; the observer must be neutral and must not become involved in the situation. When reporting back to a larger group the rules must be clear and the report back should relate to specific issues explained and agreed in advance.

Games and simulations

Games can be a useful ice-breaking activity when group members do not know one another very well, for example when a group of schools combines to run a professional training day or a conference. In a residential conference setting games can be used to help make the group gel and operate together cohesively and can concentrate on specific skills for problem-solving, team-building, promoting competition or co-operation, dependent upon the purposes of the conference. Games for team-building and co-operation can also be used by the staff of a particular school for a PTD. The use of prepared games is a way of interacting with specific ideas and information and of beginning to tackle difficult or sensitive issues such as racism and sexism.

Large-scale games and simulations do not easily fit into the format of a PTD as they are time-consuming to set up, explain and use and they normally require extended de-briefing. Large-scale games are better suited to a longer course. However, there are small games and simulations that can be used as ways into discussion and group tasks although the level of detail will determine the value of the time spent on them. Planning their use within the context of the PTD is crucial for success otherwise they become time-fillers and just a game for the participants, who will not see the relevance of the activity. Follow-up and de-briefing is essential so that the major issues of the game or simulation are brought out, discussed and used in subsequent activities.

Analysis of pupils' work

The presentation and analysis of pupils' work is a very good form of INSET. The pieces of work must be selected by the teacher concerned, according to a set of explicit criteria agreed in advance of the professional training day. Examples include how pupils' work might be assessed in relation to particular attainment targets of the national curriculum for a specific 'subject', or illustrating progression in work for a particular pupil or set of pupils. As long as the purpose has been agreed and understood the method can be a fruitful one for a PTD, and it can be combined with other issues. For example, if the school is co-operating with other schools or being visited by outsiders, the examples of pupils' work could be presented in the form of an exhibition. The process of selection and how the work selected relates to the agreed criteria would form the basis of the discussion, which must as usual be structured and led and main points of agreement or consensus recorded.

Displaying pupils' work

The process of display itself can be a useful INSET activity within a PTD with different methods of displaying children's work being demonstrated and tried out as part of the business of putting on a display for colleagues and outsiders. This method of INSET has to be used with care, as it is time-consuming to select and display work carefully. You may get useful advice from your local teachers' centre, where there is likely to be someone with long experience of selecting and displaying children's work. Criticism of pupils' work is implied criticism of the teacher concerned: the position of individual teachers must be recognized and dealt with sensitively. One way to use pupils' work is to leave them unmarked (no names or class groups) and to ask colleagues to classify them according to age and ability – in relation to national curriculum attainment targets – and then to develop criteria from that process of discussion. This could be a very good way to establish an agreed set of criteria for quality in children's work. This type of analysis is much more positive than critiques of work displayed. It can link with planning by the teachers, with some of the emphasis being on how this work was set up by the teacher concerned and what were the prior stages before this work was produced.

Analysis of the quality of work

Teachers will often instinctively agree on what makes a quality piece of work but the power of the discussion as INSET work is to make explicit the criteria used to decide upon quality and for these to be debated. To place the piece of work in the context of the ability of the pupil, the materials used, the overall work being done and, most important of all, how the teacher planned and managed the teaching and the learning environment to produce the piece of work will focus on teaching and learning and should be highly relevant as an INSET session. To move the debate on to a discussion of what quality is regardless of the particular achievement is to raise the debate still higher and is very difficult, but still worth attempting. (The use of children's work is also referred to in the section on case studies on p. 61.)

Research and projects

Traditionally these have been based on individual teacher INSET often in co-operation with higher education for the award of a degree or diploma. There is no reason why an individual who is engaged on some research should not negotiate with the headteacher and colleagues about the content of the research so that it is relevant to an important issue within the school. The use of some or part of a professional training day to present research findings to colleagues can be a very rewarding technique, especially if the research is about the school concerned. The usual issues of planning, confidentiality, the use of the information and the ownership of the research data are important and should be established in advance. When linked to higher education such activities can also provide a link between theory and practice, with the theoretical ideas being explained and illustrated by examples from the particular institution. As higher education becomes more flexible in its approach to INSET, this form of input for a PTD could increase, especially where some form of accreditation is given to individual teachers for an external award for work done within their own school.

A rich form of INSET will arise when the difficult problem of assessment of individual contributions to group work within an institution is tackled. Joint planning, execution and evaluation of a particular piece of teaching and learning by a small group of teachers, with the results of this process being presented to colleagues at a PTD, would be a useful form of INSET and a way to use case study material from the school as outlined above. Research allows in-depth work to be tackled and theory to be related to practice. Where the traditional model of individual research only is followed the results are likely to be limited and there is the possibility of someone's gaining a higher qualification and leaving the school for a promotion post. Open University courses are a convenient and useful way for teachers to engage in research and projects; the best form of such work is for a group of staff to agree on a course and join together in a block booking, which gives the advantages of flexibility of distance learning coupled with the mutual support of a group of colleagues and relevance to the work situation.

Reading

At first sight this may seem too obvious to be worth mentioning: it is, of course, a very good INSET method. Teachers are very busy people and many demands are made upon them. To reserve a time for reading can be an important, quick, easy and inexpensive INSET method. Pre-reading for PTDs can be given; it is useful to reserve some time for a quick review of reading set for a PTD to allow those who have not had time to read all the material to catch up. Reading is an efficient way for a group to be given access to particular information or ideas. The mass of information about the introduction of the national curriculum would benefit from a specific time set aside for reading the material, before going on to discuss it and its application to a particular situation. When planning a PTD there is a temptation to fill every available minute with activities, inputs and group work. Reading is a perfectly valid activity as long as it is followed up in the day. Good PTDs are well documented and handouts are often given out. Building in time on the day for participants actually to read the handouts is a valid use of INSET time. If combined with a drink before lunch or a cup of tea before the end of the day, it can provide a quiet space within a day as well as being a useful activity. Reading times can also serve as points in the day to review some of the main issues and pieces of information and be used as one means of evaluation of the day.

Using INSET packs

There is a massive expansion in the number of INSET packs being made available to schools. The Open University have for some time had a range of INSET materials for use by schools, for example *Making School-centred INSET Work* (Open University 1985). The many changes in education and the current pace of those changes as a consequence of the Education Reform Act, 1988, together with a mechanism for the delivery of school-based INSET – the five professional training days – have resulted in a deluge of INSET materials and packs on offer to schools. The CIPFA package for the introduction of local management of schools is a major and expensive package and, at a cost of £650, few individual schools will be able to afford to buy one (CIPFA 1988). The National Curriculum Council has made some INSET materials available in the form of overhead project or transparency originals and notes, *The National Curriculum Information Pack No. 1* (1989), and have produced a videotape *Developing INSET Activities* (1989). The Industrial Society (1988) have produced a videotape and notes on the Education Reform Act. Local education authorities have produced their own INSET materials and have also tried to market them to other LEAs. There is a mass of INSET material, ranging from the small and relatively cheap which schools can purchase for themselves, to free materials distributed to all schools by the National Curriculum Council, to home-produced materials from LEAs, and the major INSET packs produced by consortia of LEAs which require LEAs to take out a licence, for example the LEAP materials for management training. LEAP (Local Education Authorities Project) are currently producing a training pack for local management of schools (LEAP 1990). The range of materials on offer, the differences in quality and costs, the licences taken out by different LEAs and the different materials produced by LEAs themselves, all combine to make a very confusing picture for schools who wish to consider what is available, and – more importantly – what materials exist to support their particular INSET programme and even more importantly how to make the best use of what is available. The first point of contact as to what is available in any particular LEA is the INSET adviser or inspector, the INSET co-ordinator and the local teachers' centre staff.

Once what is on offer is known, the use of these packs of INSET material can be planned. It is unlikely to be effective simply to buy an INSET pack or to book one for loan and use it cold on a PTD. The INSET packs are all produced at a general level and cannot possibly take account of particular local LEA and school needs. The INSET packs are a useful resource but their use has to be planned into a school programme; selection of the packs and of which parts to use has to be made by the person planning and running the particular PTD. It may be possible to book the services of an advisory teacher who has used the packs and who can help with the planning, but it is essential that the person organizing the day knows the materials and decides what parts of the pack will be used and how they will be used. If this selection and planning is not done, it is similar to asking an expert to come in and lecture without briefing them in advance or planning their input into a day. INSET packs are a response to the need for materials to support change in schools but their use has to be carefully planned in exactly the same way as all other INSET activities. The temptation of the designers of some packs is to attempt to make them 'teacher proof'. This is based on a deficit model of schools and teachers and will not lead to INSET which promotes change.

Videotapes

Many of the INSET packs contain video material and the use of videotapes is a popular INSET activity. It can be a good way to present information and ideas, but can be abused within INSET activities. Some videotapes present information and ideas, others give an insight into particular aspects of schools, classrooms and teaching. To sit and watch a videotape for its whole duration is seldom a useful INSET activity. The person planning the session must watch the videotape before the event and select clips which should be used according to the purpose of the day, either to give information or to make a particular point. Where a videotape is used to give insight into particular schools and classrooms it must be remembered that it is a selection by someone else, giving only a partial view. Good videotapes are accompanied by notes which make this clear and give the background and the motives. When using this type of material the viewers should be asked to observe particular things shown and to comment on what they have seen, according to the plan for the PTD and the points you wish to bring out. To use a videotape in this way promotes discussion and small groups can be asked to compare impressions and observations. Once this is done, the video clip can be reshown for the viewers to check their initial reactions in the light of their discussions with colleagues.

Home-produced videotapes

It is easy to use modern video cameras to produce videotapes of classroom activity, but it is time-consuming and the final product will, of course, be the result of editing by someone with a particular view. The use of home-produced videotapes can be very revealing as they are observations of teaching and learning in a highly relevant situation but they have the same dangers as the case studies from within the school (see p. 61).

Plenary and reporting back

Reporting back to a larger group the results of small group work frequently appears on INSET programmes. These sessions are often dull, repetitive and of very little use. The common pattern is for a verbal report by the leader of a group (or the person pressed into this role by fellow group members). At INSET sessions the participants normally do want feedback about other groups; it is tempting to forgo the reporting back but this is not popular and is not a good idea as participants are denied access to the work of others. If the school has been working on a particular problem, the report back and planning the next step are essential.

There are ways to make reporting back more interesting and manageable. Small groups producing written material for others is one method which cuts down the amount of description of what went on, give access to ideas and promotes comparison and discussion. The written report can be on sheets of paper under certain prearranged headings or in the form of a grid, a chart, a diagram or anything to organize the ideas and restrict them to usable form. If the report is in the form of flip-chart notes pinned up for all to see, it should be a summary of the discussions rather than the notes made at the time. It will be helpful if the reports are presented in similar ways by all the groups, using prearranged headings and format so that comparisons are easy to make. The review of the work of other groups can take place immediately before a break so that everyone is asked to look at or read the reports and an agenda is given for the discussion to follow.

Organizing the report back can make these sessions more stimulating. Sharing the task of reporting back gives variety as well as preventing certain individuals from dominating the process. Ideas for reporting back can be that more than one person has to be involved in the report back; the report back must take no longer than a given time; the report back should contain several styles (some written, some oral, and others, such as pictorial, role play, interview, press release). The report back can be reduced in length and refined by allowing observers from other groups to join in at certain points to get access to the thinking of others as the work progresses instead of leaving it all to the end.

The final report back must be well chaired. Instead of taking the whole of a report from one group the chair can ask all the groups to address a different point in turn using a prepared agenda which all can see. Questions should be limited to points of fact and discussion allowed only after the report back and in the way planned. Agreements must be recorded and written up for future use. The common practice of promising to record everything and reproduce it for everyone is very wasteful: summaries and highlights for future use are by far the best approach.

Commercial organizations

There have always been educational manufacturers, publishers and distributors who have offered schools and teachers INSET sessions. LEA policy on these sessions has varied and there has always been suspicion about sales sessions. The overall climate of education is changing and education is being exhorted to co-operate with industry and commerce. Some of the offers from commercial organizations have always been very good and will continue to be so. Selling is often indirect through the use of particular equipment and materials, and such sessions are often backed up by small exhibitions. It is unlikely that commercial organizations would wish to become involved in the professional training day of an individual school but they may well be interested to do so with a group of schools or at a centre where there is an exhibition of their products. This can be a cheap way to run INSET as often the company will provide materials and speakers free of charge. As with all other forms of INSET the day must be planned, and if the offer of a commercial organization is relevant it can be planned into the day, the company can be briefed and an agreement reached which is acceptable to both sides without any direct or pressure selling. Where the topic for the INSET day is to do with school-industry links, there will obviously be benefits in co-operation with commercial organizations. Ideally the company representatives who take part in the session should include people with teaching experience who have used the materials or equipment in the classroom. Certainly the jobs of the people from the organization should be known and their motives made explicit. Some firms will leave equipment or materials for use in the school as part of a pilot project: not only will the school acquire free items, but also the evaluation of the materials used will have potential INSET use.

Summary of some of the major INSET methods and techniques

This section summarizes some of the INSET methods and techniques described and may be photocopied (as also may the planning sheets in Chapter 4 and the evaluation methods summaries in Chapter 5) and used as an aid to planning a PTD.

CONFERENCES

Conferences may be for a day or longer periods of time. Residential conferences are a good way to bring a group together, introduce change and build a team; they are likely to take place wholly or partly at weekends.

For	*Against*
• good with larger groups	• costly in time and money
• can confer status on PTDs	• good venue essential

For
- residential conferences a powerful way to bring about change

Against
- domestic situations may prevent participation by some teachers

Examples

A cluster of schools meets together for a day conference and shares costs before following up the conference with school-based INSET. A whole staff joins a residential conference to formulate a new policy.

VISITS AND OBSERVATION

Visits are most valuable if made in school time but can take place outside school time. Visits can be made to one's own school. Visits must be carefully prepared and followed up. Visits do not have to be made only to schools of excellence. Visits need not be for the whole staff on the same day and do not have to take up the entire day.

For
- relevant to teaching and learning
- encourages comparison with own situation
- popular with teachers
- good for fact-finding

Against
- can produce superficial tips only
- can be threatening to receiving teacher
- time-consuming, good preparation essential
- visitors change the situation

Examples

Teachers visit other schools to see how computers are organized, used and integrated into the curriculum and report back on a wide range of different situations before deciding on policy for their own school. Reciprocal visits are made to each other's classrooms by teachers at the same primary school as part of a whole school policy to organize classrooms along similar principles.

MEETINGS

Meetings can be used to reach consensus, generate alternatives and take decisions.

For
- integrates INSET into school life

Against
- wastes time if only for giving information

For	*Against*
• focus for decisions and use of INSET	• 'Oh no, not another meeting'

Examples
Staff meet to discuss plans for a PTD and decide who takes responsibility for organizing various aspects. Department meeting decides upon new practice as the result of dissemination of INSET visits.

LECTURES

Lectures are a traditional form of INSET appropriate to a large group who quickly need access to information, theory and the experience of others.

For	*Against*
• access for audience to an expert	• teachers in a passive role
• inexpensive, especially for large groups	• inefficient as concentration spans short
• can be an excellent stimulus for a day	• much time necessary for briefing speaker

Examples
A senior LEA inspector contributes to a PTD on national curriculum with a talk about retaining existing good practice. A lecture on local management of schools sets out the facts as in the DES circular and suggests ways to think them through for a specific school situation.

WORKSHOPS

Workshops involve small groups in some practical activity which leads to a product, such as experience of a teaching method, use of certain learning resources, physically making materials or producing a set of ideas. Workshops use the experience of their members within a structured set of activities.

For	*Against*
• participants involved and experience used	• time-consuming for detailed planning
• the product can be used in the school	• where items are used or made, materials can be expensive

Examples
Primary teachers use tools and materials to make working models and discuss a range of teaching strategies for incorporating technology into planned project work. Secondary teachers work on plans for a videotape on drugs education before using the ideas with students.

GROUP WORK

Group work covers a wide variety of activities, which are characterized by small numbers of participants who are involved in a carefully planned and structured activity, although the group will take control of events. Group work uses the experience of the members to complete a task and the results of group work are shared with other groups. Activities include brainstorming, paired and small group discussion.

For
- involves all participants if well planned
- practical and relevant to teaching
- allows time to explore concepts or skills with colleagues in depth
- gives access to each other's experience

Against
- time for planning and preparation essential
- difficulty in choosing group members
- some groups work better than others
- difficulty of managing effective reporting back

Examples
Individuals write down their concept of quality in children's work, share it with a colleague and then in a small group discussion refine the task and produce a list of elements of quality work which are related to the school's planning and record-keeping practice. Two departments in a secondary school decide on their joint and separate contributions to teaching for certain attainment targets for the national curriculum.

CASE STUDIES

For
- relevant and interesting materials

Against
- effort to preserve confidentiality

For
- with specific cases can result in action

Against
- commercial cases are expensive and may be seen as irrelevant

Example
A group of teachers works through materials on child abuse, relates it to cases at the school in the past and decides upon policy and responsibilities.

ROLE PLAY

For
- can change attitudes
- involves participants
- can lead to understanding of other points of view
- a good way to tackle sensitive issues
- can be fun

Against
- can be threatening
- time for careful planning
- difficult to share experience with those not involved
- needs time to be effective

Example
Pastoral staff at a secondary school each take role of teacher, pupil and parent in turn to look at different perspectives and possible action to resolve a complaint against the school about a racist incident.

4
Planning in detail

Introduction

Planning is essential for the success of any INSET activity. The professional training day should be located within an overall school INSET policy so that it relates to other INSET activities. When planning a PTD, using a check-list or a planning sheet will help. The check-list here is copyright-free: you may photocopy it for your personal use. The headings are explained in detail in this chapter, which ends with some examples of planning sheets which you may also copy or adapt for your own use (pp. 85–93).

The planning and running of a PTD is both time-consuming and difficult: delegating various jobs to colleagues will not only make the task more manageable but also involve other participants in their day.

Check-list for planning a professional training day

1 Schools
2 Dates
3 Venues
4 Aims
5 Objectives
6 Times and detailed timetable
7 Organization of groups

8 Rooms and layout
9 Equipment
10 Materials
11 Inputs
12 Domestic arrangements
13 Administrative details
14 Planning for problems
15 Summary and analysis of timetable
16 Who is doing what?
17 Details for publication
18 Evaluation

Schools

If you are planning a joint INSET you should record the names of all the schools involved, including, of course, your own school. If only a part of the PTD is to be shared, you should define the extent of every school's involvement in the various activities.

Dates

When the dates have been agreed, specify both the day of the week and the date. Mistakes occasionally occur and this will help to avoid confusion and highlight any errors. Check published dates and inform everyone immediately if any changes need to be made.

Venues

If part or all of the PTD is to be held away from the school, all participants must be given the full address and telephone number of the venue, a map showing its location, travelling details (including public transport and parking facilities) and a clear site plan. The PTD organizer must ensure that all the participants know where to go and how to get there; arrange for members of staff to share cars if necessary. Give clear instructions on who to ask for at the venue and which room to go to for the start of the session (which obviously you will need to organize beforehand). If the participants' travelling expenses are payable, arrange in advance what is allowed and the procedure for claiming; inform all the participants, preferably in writing. This task can be delegated.

Keep notes of all travelling expenses and any costs to do with the venue.

Aims

The overall aims of the PTD together with links to past INSET, school INSET policy and intended links to subsequent INSET should be carefully defined. Links to other school policies should be included. An edited version of the aims for the day should appear in the publicity material.

Objectives

A list of detailed objectives for the day should be written down. These will help in planning the day as a practical event, fitting in the activities and timetabling them. Do not be tempted to produce too many objectives: the more precise they are the better. The list of detailed objectives will vary for every PTD, but when planning professional training days build in the opportunity for participants to contribute and use their own experience and skills through reflection and discussion of good practice. The chance to relate what has been learned to their own work must also be planned into the day and linked with evaluation. Objectives specified in advance are a great aid to monitoring the success of the day as it progresses and will enable slight changes to be made; together with a statement of the aims they will help the process of evaluation. It is almost impossible to organize an effective PTD without specifying objectives and having a detailed plan. Paradoxically it is much easier to modify a detailed plan in the course of a PTD than it is to respond to feedback without a specific plan. Evaluation of the INSET, the day itself and the learning which has taken place should appear as one of the objectives, and time for evaluation and suggestions for subsequent INSET should be in the timetable.

Times and detailed timetable

The start and finish times must be clearly stated and strictly observed. A detailed time plan must be made with all time in the day carefully planned and accounted for. Inevitably it will not work out exactly but it will give a clear framework which will enable changes as the day develops much easier to make. The detailed time plan ought not to be used as the PTD programme, but will be used by the organizer and helpers for particular sessions. The detailed plan should be observed for the overall shape of the day, which will be dictated by the domestic breaks. This plan can be analysed to show the amount of time spent on organization, domestic breaks, contact time for participants and the amount of time teachers are actively involved, so that the plan can be modified as necessary. Unless the teachers are actively involved for at least 50 per cent of the day, the INSET is unlikely to be effective. Some of the case studies in Chapter 2 have been analysed on the basis of time spent in different modes of activity and involvement to illustrate this.

Organization of groups

In drawing up the timetable it will be possible to see what activities are planned for groups of teachers as well as how much time is to be devoted to group work activities. Allocation of participants to groups, allocation of groups to rooms, the materials and equipment the groups will need, leadership of the groups and specific tasks for the groups should all be planned in advance. The published time-table will show the arrangement of group work and the times allo-cated, which avoids much confusion and time-wasting of getting into groups on the day. When the day is being held away from the school, the person in charge of the venue will need to know the number and nature of the group rooms required; the group rooms should be specified on the timetable.

Rooms and layout

The planning of group activities will determine the number and size of rooms required. The equipment needed for the PTD, the space it requires and the number of participants will determine the layouts for the rooms. Do draw plans: it is usually worth the effort. The arrangement of the furniture in the room will have a strong effect on the way that a group operates. Chairs grouped round tables with papers and pens laid out ready implies a very different working atmosphere from a number of easy chairs arranged in a circle, or from several straight rows of chairs all facing the front. Arrange the furniture to suit your purpose. If you are planning a session which uses video material, it will be doomed to failure if some of the audience cannot see the television screen. Do check all the sight-lines in advance.

Equipment

Make a list of what equipment is required for the PTD, including anything which a visiting speaker has requested to be provided. It will probably include items of audio-visual hardware such as video-recorders, tape-recorders, television monitors, overhead projectors and slide projectors. Make arrangements for these to be available on the day and ensure that they can all be used in the rooms allocated (check the number of socket outlets and whether extension leads are needed). If possible have spare bulbs and back-up machines to hand. You can delegate the responsibility for organizing these items. If the PTD is being held outside the school, discuss details of what equipment is needed with the person providing it at the venue.

Other equipment may be needed, such as flip-charts, display boards, specialist equipment such as computers and science equipment, and tools for workshops. Everything should be listed. The job of collecting the equipment together and ensuring that it is available and functioning in the right place at the right time can be delegated; this also helps the day to run smoothly as time is not wasted while equipment is fetched, set up and made to work. If outside speakers are contributing to the day they should be asked well in advance what equipment they will bring with them and what you have to provide for them. Access to a photocopier, on what basis and its cost should be considered in advance. All equipment costs should be noted.

Materials

A list of materials required should be compiled from the detailed timetable: the task of collecting them together and making them available at the PTD can be delegated to a colleague. Having all the necessary materials ready when they are required avoids wasting time on the day. Costs of the materials should be noted.

Inputs

If outside speakers are being used they will have to be briefed in detail and the session planned into the day. Why is this person being used? Has the speaker been recommended? What will be the cost? What are the speaker's correct details: role, status, base, address, telephone number? The use of other inputs such as hand-out material and videotapes will need to be reviewed in advance. Note all expenses incurred.

Domestic arrangements

INSET days are different and special: the domestic arrangements for the day can help make the day successful. Provision of tea, coffee and lunch can be delegated in advance. If funds are available lunch could be provided, perhaps with a glass of wine, plus non-alcoholic beverages. The domestic breaks at PTDs are important and often the discussion of the INSET continues in the breaks; this is less likely to happen if some teachers go to the nearest pub while others stay in the staffroom to eat sandwiches. If possible, keep the whole group together on the premises where the PTD is being held, and provide lunch for them at a modest (or no) cost in a way that is very different from a normal school day. If several members of staff are willing to prepare and serve a simple lunch this is a reasonable compromise. However, it should not always be the same teachers who provide the lunch and on mixed sex staff it should not always be the women teachers who organize lunch. When the day is being run out of school, the domestic arrangements should be planned by the organizer in conjunction with the venue. Make a note of the costs of lunch and other breaks.

Administrative details

It is essential to keep detailed notes of all the expenses and total them, determine the source of funds and agree them with the head-teacher or the member of staff responsible. Collect any forms necessary such as registers and claim forms. Produce handouts in advance and a list of what they are. Keep a file copy of any letters of confirmation to an outside speaker or staff at an external venue. Arrange for any payments to be made to speakers, external venues, for provision of lunches, etc. Prepare and circulate the publicity for the day. Prepare an evaluation sheet which can be used on the day by the participants.

One of the most helpful things about professional training days is the lack of interruptions and the use of a sustained period of time for the INSET work. If the PTD is going to be held on site, try to ensure that there will be no outside interruptions. Ask the school secretary, one of the helpers or a parent to answer any telephone calls and take messages, or be a first line of coping with any visitors. Perhaps using an answer phone would help prevent distractions. Ensure that the PTD starts promptly so that busy teachers do not become involved in their day-to-day work.

Planning for problems

Latecomers

Always start on time but plan in advance how to deal with the inevitable latecomers: they must not be allowed to disrupt the flow of the day. Avoid the temptation to be sarcastic or annoyed and never interact with the details of the excuse for lateness. Try hard to welcome them to the group, briefly explain what is happening and incorporate them as quickly as possible. Have ready the detailed timetable so the latecomers can see what is going on and what is expected of them, and give them their handouts to date. If the latecomers arrive when the participants are in small groups, place them in their groups and ask members of the group to explain where they are in their work. If the whole group is together, it may be a good moment to recap briefly for the benefit of the whole group as well as the latecomers.

Dominators, cynics and comics

There can be participants who tend to dominate discussions. When organizing a PTD for your own staff, you will know who these people are likely to be: plan accordingly. Give these people a role which is likely to keep them busy, e.g. note-maker, the person who has to summarize a series of flip-chart notes and produce a legible copy for later discussion or presentation, or the person who ensures the rules of the particular activity are enforced, especially if this is in the form of individual work building up to pairs and larger groups. The structure of the day where everyone has the opportunity to be actively involved will reduce the chance for a few individuals to dominate.

Occasionally there will be disruptive participants, for example the staffroom cynic who has seen it all before. Again, when planning a PTD for your own staff you will know who these people will be and you must plan to deal with them. The main strategy is to isolate disruptive people and bring pressure on them to conform and participate. Enlist the help of the other members of the group to stay on task and if necessary work with the disruptive ones yourself. Comics can be very useful as long as they are not allowed to play to the audience too much: the humour can be used to diffuse difficult situations just as it can ruin sensitive ones. The emphasis in the planning of involvement, with participants' having a clear structure with definite tasks, will help to minimize the disruption and is likely to get the group on your side, bringing pressure on the disruptive ones to conform and join in with the tasks.

Summary and analysis of timetable

Do a breakdown of the timetable to show how much time is spent on the INSET activities themselves, how much on organization and how much on domestic arrangements; decide for how long the teachers will be actively involved in the INSET and how much time they will be passive. Use this information to see the shape of the day: ensure there are varied activities and changes of pace. This preliminary analysis will probably result in changes to the plans for the day. Check that for every category someone has agreed to ensure that the activity will take place. What will participants be expected to do before the day and what will they be expected to bring with them to the day. To see the overall shape of the day, write times in minutes under headings:

1 Active
2 Passive
3 Administration
4 Domestic breaks
5 Total

Who is doing what?

Planning and arranging a PTD is very time-consuming. Delegating responsibility for various aspects of the organization to colleagues will not only ease your work-load but also increase participation by those teachers for whom the INSET is intended. Keep clear notes of the tasks for which each member of staff is responsible, and make sure that they give you details of any expenses incurred.

Details for publication

Publicity material for the PTD should be circulated among all the participants. It should include dates, venue, times and a brief description of the aims and objectives of the INSET. Nearer the day the participants should be given full details of activities planned for the PTD, the administrative, organizational and domestic arrangements, and any preparation they are required to do plus a list of anything they should bring with them. The detailed timetable will need to be available to participants on the day, together with handouts and evaluation sheets. You should plan what documentation and final reports will be issued after the PTD has taken place.

Evaluation

Evaluation is integral to planning and the aims and objectives specified in advance. Decide what will count as success for the day and how you will know. Avoid the temptation to concentrate narrowly upon the events of the day itself: the venue, the quality of the speaker and value for money of the food are all important, but the real questions are to do with what has been learned, how this will affect teaching and what will be planned for subsequent INSET. Produce a brief set of questions for evaluation and build time for evaluation into the day. PTDs are a significant resource and the temptation is to fill them with as much INSET activity as possible, with evaluation as an afterthought or crammed into the end of the day. Monitoring and evaluation are crucial for success and both need time. A review of the morning can provide feedback which results in modification of the afternoon's planned programme. (Evaluation is dealt with in detail in Chapter 5.)

Planning is vital to success; INSET days are unlikely all to be perfectly organized and run, and will not all be exceptional events. However, they must be well planned, organized and run otherwise the participants will be justifiably annoyed at the waste of their time.

Planning sheets for professional training days

_____

Schools

Organizer_____   _____

Dates_____ Start time_____ Finish time_____

Venues

Liaison _____

Aims

Include links to school development plan and past and future INSET.

Objectives

What does the PTD set out to achieve?

_____

Detailed timetable for organizer

Account for all the time in the PTD.	Structure timings round breaks.
9.00	start
10.00	
11.00	coffee
12.00	
1.00	lunch
2.00	
3.00	tea
4.00	
5.00	finish

Organization of groups

_____

Composition of groups
Leaders
Activities
Different groupings
Activities

Who?

_____

Rooms and layout

_____

Plans
Groups in which rooms
Equipment in rooms
Materials in rooms
Layout of furniture

Who?

_____

Equipment

Television monitor
Video-recorder
Tape-recorder
Overhead projector
Slide projector
Flip-charts
Display boards
Computers
Tools
Photocopier

Who?

Materials

Handouts
Paper
Card
Pens and pencils
Scissors
Glue
Books

Who?

Inputs

Handouts
Videotapes
OHP transparencies
Slides

Outside speakers
Name/status
Address/phone
Base
Role
Briefed
Visited
Equipment

Who?

Domestic arrangements

Staff travel arrangements
Coffee break
Lunch
Tea break

Who?

Administrative details

Expenses
Venue
Travel
Equipment
Materials
Inputs
Beverages
Lunch

Total expenses _____

Source of funds

Registers
Claim forms

Who?

Summary and analysis of timetable

Participants and their role
Active
Passive
Administration
Domestic
Pace and variety of activities
Relevance to needs
Advance preparation by participants
Items to be provided by participants
Review and modify plan as necessary

Who is doing what?

Venue
Group organization
Room layouts
Equipment
Materials
Inputs
Travel arrangements
Travel expenses
Coffee/tea breaks
Lunch
Telephone/visitors

Details for publication

Participants will need to know in advance the following details, including information on what will happen and what they have to do:

Dates
Times
Venue
Rooms
Aims and objectives
Timetable summary
Group activities
Domestic arrangements
Who to contact

On the day
Detailed timetables
Handouts
Evaluation sheets

After the day
Documentation
Final reports

Evaluation

How will you know if it has worked?

On the day

In the long term

Refer back to aims and objectives

What next?

Organizer's comments

How well did it work?

What next?

Simplified planning sheet for professional training days

Times   Total time available
Venue   Rooms
Dates   Cost

Aims

Objectives

Timetable Activities   Equipment/MATERIALS   Who does what?

Room layouts

Evaluation

Activities: range/variety/pace

Timings: active/passive

5
Evaluation

We take it as axiomatic that evaluation ought to be a component of every in-service enterprise: this view is not universally spread throughout the teaching force. It is likely that the case for an evaluation of a PTD will have to be argued and it is important to be clear about some of the issues.

Why evaluate?

1 To make improvements in future PTDs so that they are more effective and more enjoyable (probably the most important reason).
2 To provide data that will assist the development of other INSET activities.
3 To identify future needs and topics for INSET.
4 To enable participants to enhance their own learning.
5 For reasons of accountability: to whom?
6 For the LEA, to demonstrate value for money.
7 To judge the cost-effectiveness of the day.
8 To establish whether the aims and objectives were achieved.
9 To discover the impact of the day on classroom practice.
10 To find out if it was a worthwhile enterprise educationally.

Who will be involved in the evaluation?

1 All the members of staff in the school?

2   Only the teachers who participated in the PTD?
3   Only the organizers of the PTD?
4   Only those who made a contribution to the PTD?
5   Will an external agent be asked to evaluate the PTD?
6   Who will have access to the results of the evaluation (and why)?

What will be evaluated?

Daniel Stufflebeam *et al.* (1971) suggest four kinds of evaluation: input, output, process, context.

Input

The purpose of input evaluation is to 'provide information for determining how to utilize resources to meet program goals' (Stufflebeam *et al*. 1971). That is, how will you use the people and materials you have to achieve the objectives you seek?

Output

Product evaluation focuses on the extent to which objectives were (or were not) achieved.

Process

Process evaluation is concerned with implementation, and building up an interpretive description of the process, an account of 'what actually happened'. This process resembles what Parlett and Hamilton (1972) call 'illuminative evaluation'.

Context

Context evaluation analyses the situation, describing and defining actual and desired conditions; it questions the value of any stated goals and looks for 'unmet needs' and 'unused opportunities'.

Consideration of these four dimensions might offer a useful way for a school to examine the evaluation of a PTD. Teachers will want to avoid doing something merely for its own sake, and Stufflebeam's analysis can help focus attention upon the particular aspect which evaluation is mainly required to illuminate.

What use will be made of the evaluation?

The main use should be to support the needs of the school, teachers and pupils, but there will be some external agencies who will legitimately require some information. It would be useful to ascertain, in advance of any INSET activities, the nature of the information needed. If the internal needs of the school are appropriately addressed, there should be sufficient data for purposes of accountability. This whole question is related to that of 'Who is it for?', and – for different constituencies – evaluation has come to include accountability and accounting. Full discussion of these aspects is beyond the scope of this book, but organizers of PTDs in schools need to be aware of such issues, and some elements of them are explored in the next section.

How will the evaluation be carried out?

Before deciding this, it is necessary to think through some of the issues in order to better evaluate the day. 'How?' will be influenced by the kinds of responses you have made to the 'Why?', 'Who?' and 'What?' questions. Some suggestions are given at the end of this chapter. To serve 'these various interests might require different kinds of evaluation methods and the responsibility for some of these is likely to lie outside the school. The staff development tutor or other responsible member of staff should have some awareness of what is happening elsewhere *vis-à-vis* evaluation. The requirements of the LEA (and probably of the DES) can usually be met by the production of an account of the activities. This should identify how resources have been used and how that use was appropriate (and legitimate). Where there are people in the Authority who wish to see a more in-depth evaluation they would normally contact the school directly.

The main thrust of the 'educational' evaluation should explore how the PTD might have been handled differently in order to make it more effective, as well as its impact upon teachers and pupils. It is important to plan sufficient *time* and *resources* into the PTD activities for the purposes of evaluation. It will be, for all intents and purposes an internal document, and this will be the case whether the evaluation is conducted by an external agent (see Chapter 6 for a discussion of the use of external people) or by members of staff. In any event, a key component of the process will be self-evaluation.

Evaluation on the day by the participants

There are various methods of doing this. The participants can be divided into groups (no fewer than three, no more than eight) and their responses to the evaluation questions noted on a flip-chart. Using flip-charts lets all the group see the points being made, which helps both accuracy and consensus. (Flip-charts are sometimes used for frivolous or inappropriate reasons: the pads of paper are quite expensive and ought not to be wasted on irrelevant or ill-thought-out scribbles!)

A suggested list of questions for the groups to consider is

1 What would you like to say about the day?
2 What were the high points and the low points?
3 Which aspects had most relevance?
4 What kind of follow-up would you like?

Another suggestion is to list as many criteria by which you would judge the value of the day to

1 the participants
2 the pupils
3 the school as a whole

and then evaluate the day using these criteria.

Evaluation by the INSET co-ordinator or staff development tutor

1 The co-ordinator or tutor should be given the reports made by the participants in their evaluation sessions.
2 Questionnaires should be given to the participants as soon as possible (preferably during the PTD itself) and should include the question 'What next?'
3 The staff development tutor or external agent, present as an observer, can produce an account of the PTD. (Some aspects of this kind of evaluation are explored in the rest of this chapter.)
4 Structured interviews can be conducted with a sample of staff. These can be (but need not always be) time-consuming, but in some cases they offer a means of gaining insights into staff perceptions that other methods might not achieve.
5 'Action plans' can be negotiated with individuals and groups of staff.

Purposes of evaluation

It can be argued that it is possible to have adequate monitoring and evaluation if evaluation is part of the INSET activities and not something tagged on at a later time. One of the reasons why evaluation is carried out is to enhance the participants' own learning. This point is well made by Easterby-Smith (1986), who gives three main purposes of evaluation:

1 Proving, which aims to 'demonstrate conclusively that something has happened' as a result of staff development.
2 Improving, which seeks to ensure that 'programmes become better than they are'.
3 Learning, which recognizes that 'evaluation cannot . . . be divorced from the processes upon which it concentrates'.

These purposes are, of course, interrelated but we would argue strongly for the primacy of *learning*. To engage in such a process of learning requires close interaction between the participants at all levels, including those responsible for the evaluation.

We shall now review various methods of evaluation.

Questionnaires

Questionnaires should preferably be administered and completed within the time-span of the PTD, in order to ensure an accurate and comprehensive response. Care is needed when framing questions: they should be short but unambiguous. Questionnaires should be used in conjunction with other methods of evaluation.

Advantages

1 Useful for obtaining an immediate overview.
2 Quick and efficient feedback from large numbers of participants (invaluable when several schools are sharing a PTD).
3 Standardized structure for the responses.

Disadvantages

1 Quantitative rather than qualitative data are generated.
2 Information supplied is often superficial.
3 Problem of how best to use the information obtained.

Interviews

Interviews are usually the most appropriate form of evaluation. They require adequate preparation by both interviewer and interviewee, each of whom should clearly understand and accept the ground-rules. It is recommended that interviewers receive some training in this method.

Advantages

1 Useful for obtaining in-depth qualitative data.
2 Invaluable when the issues are not very clear.
3 Interviewing enables 'probing'.

Disadvantages

1 Tend to be very time-consuming without appropriate training and careful preparation.
2 Badly conducted interviews have a very negative effect.
3 Some responses can be difficult to record.

Group discussions

Discussions require skilled handling by the group's leader: perhaps training for leaders might be a prerequisite.

Advantages

1 Quick and simple to organize on the day.
2 Useful for obtaining an immediate impression.

Disadvantages

1 Discussion can be difficult to record and to analyse.
2 Without skilled leadership discussion can be unproductive.

Action plans

Action plans are follow-up activities which are built into the planning of the PTD. The completion date for these should be agreed during the PTD. Action plans are particularly effective if they involve an undertaking by various members of staff to meet at specified intervals in order to produce documentation which encapsulates a particular topic (see for example the case study on staff appraisal, pp. 39–44).

Advantages

1 Help to make links between PTD activities and classroom practice.
2 Assist participants in being forward-looking.
3 Useful for identifying priorities for the school.
4 Locate potential difficulties in the path of implementation.

Disadvantages

1 Could be viewed as merely an exercise on paper (this will be influenced by previous experiences in the school).
2 Further meetings imply a commitment which may be unwelcome to some busy teachers.

Observation

Observation here means the observation by a non-participant at the PTD itself. (Observation in the classroom of the effects of the INSET activities is another valid method of evaluation: it can be one teacher observing another, teachers observing pupils, or teachers monitoring their own practice by using a video camera.) Although it is possible to obtain useful evaluation from one of the participants of the PTD, it is much more valuable to have as an observer someone who is not participating in the activities. This could be one of the school's members of staff, who will need clear briefing on the skills required for this role and a firm agreement solely to observe, not participate; otherwise the INSET consultant (if you are using one – see Chapter 6) may be prepared to act in that capacity or be able to suggest a suitable neutral outsider as a 'critical friend'.

Advantages

1 A clear and detailed description of the day highlights for the participants how they spent (or intended to spend) their time.
2 The observer may see aspects of the day not recognized by the participants.

3 Unintended outcomes can more easily be recorded and assessed.
4 Particular aspects of the context of the INSET can be explored (e.g. Were equal opportunities issues adequately addressed?).

Disadvantages

1 The nature and purpose of the INSET activity need to be very carefully negotiated.
2 The development of both trust and competence takes time.
3 Direct observation implies collaboration; many teachers have not had the opportunity to spend time developing appropriate skills.

Outcomes

What should we hope for from the evaluation? What would count as success? Various indicators have emerged in our work with teachers:

1 Effect on pupil learning.
2 Effect on staff morale.
3 Some sense of an end product.
4 Identifiable 'school improvement'.
5 Relevance (e.g. related to the SDP).
6 Consultation in the choice of theme.
7 Involvement in the way in which it was done.
8 Participation in the day itself.
9 Collaboration in the evaluation.
10 Did it address a *real* priority?
11 Did it relieve any pressure?

In so far as you think that these factors are important, you may wish to see that they are addressed in the evaluation.

6
The use of external agencies and resources

Do you need them?

On most occasions, schools are left to their own devices and there is rarely the chance to use other than their own resources. Often these are more than adequate; sometimes they are the best available. Some schools are too easily inclined to rush and obtain the services of an 'outside speaker' as if, by definition, the quality of the INSET would be higher. It may well be that the best resources for a particular need are within the school itself; certainly attempts should be made to utilize the strengths residing in the school. Members of staff with a designated staff development role may well be up to the tasks of planning, running, or making a contribution to a PTD. One of the jobs of a staff development tutor is to identify and encourage other teachers who could make a worthwhile contribution.

There are many in-service programmes on offer – by colleges, polytechnics, institutes of education and teachers' centres – which are aimed at the staff development tutor and designed to present some of the knowledge and skills needed for the planning, delivery and evaluation of INSET. Key personnel from the school could, with profit, participate in some of these.

The role of the consultant

Having recognized the need to use suitable resources found within the school, there is also little doubt that many in-school activities could benefit from the process of 'consultancy'. This (overworked) title is used to label a wide range of personnel. We shall use the term 'consultant' merely to mean a person used by the school to facilitate an activity or set of activities. Thus a consultant may come from the ranks of the staff (and not necessarily, although admittedly usually, from the senior management).

It is worth distinguishing (Gough 1976) between task-consultancy and process-consultancy. In the INSET field generally there is a significant place for task-consultancy, but we would suggest that for PTDs the primary need is usually for a process-consultant. This need arises at all stages of the process: preparatory and planning operations, structuring the day itself, delivery and evaluation.

A consultant who is not brought in early enough might be constrained in that initial decisions have already determined the nature and direction of events. It is likely (if the consultant is any good) that time and effort will be saved and unfortunate choices obviated. Even at the early stage of selecting a topic or theme, discussion with a consultant can prove useful. For example, schools often attempt to achieve too much in a day; it is frustrating when either a great deal is covered superficially, or some aspects are dealt with sketchily or not at all. An experienced consultant will help you focus the theme more specifically. Perhaps the topic you have identified is contingent upon other knowledge and skills which have not been addressed, or – more usually – there would be merit in clarifying some issues about X, before embarking upon a PTD dealing with Y. For example, there would be little point in spending a day on the computerization of pupil records until there was agreement about what records were to be kept and for what purposes.

Having specified a theme with some precision, a consultant should be helpful in suggesting ways in which this might be approached on the day. Certainly we would expect a consultant to be able to indicate a range of options available, including the identification of appropriate resources in terms of both materials and personnel. Alternative suggestions to the 'talk–discussion–talk–discussion' mode should be advocated, and perhaps more ways in which members of staff can actively participate in the sessions. The consultant should help you determine specifically what the intended outcomes of the day are, and offer some suggestions on how the day might be evaluated. In some cases, a school may have built a longer term relationship with a consultant and thus planning for a PTD will be part of a wider programme with which the consultant is involved.

In any event, it is important that the consultant should focus upon the needs and wishes of the school, rather than become engaged in a topic of personal interest. It has to be made clear from the start that the consultant is there on the school's terms. There are too many cases of schools being led in directions different from their own intentions and inclinations (rather like the boy scout who helped the old lady across the road when she didn't want to go). This implies some form of contract: while not necessarily taking the form of a formal document (although it would be no bad thing if it did), it should involve a negotiated agreement. During this process of negotiation the school should make very clear what its expectations are; the consultant is, of course, free to accept or reject the conditions. Here the consultant can be very helpful in aiding the clarification of the issues for the benefit and understanding of both parties.

The consultant may play an active part in the day itself: perhaps giving some kind of presentation, or facilitating group work, or being a non-participant observer as part of the evaluation process. The consultant may not need to be involved in the PTD itself, but in this case there should be an account of the day so that the consultant is aware of what happened. Any evaluation will, of course, be available; there may also be minutiae of the day which could be of relevance to the consultant but which might not emerge in the evaluation. Wherever possible, it is suggested that the consultant should be present and, particularly if making a significant contribution, should not carry out the evaluation. If another external person is brought in for the evaluation, the planning for this should be part of the process of negotiation. (Other possibilities regarding the use of outside people for evaluation are discussed on pp. 98–102.)

What to look for in a consultant

Consultancy is threatening to become education's biggest growth industry ('The fastest vehicle in a vacuum is a bandwagon' – Thornbury 1972) and you should have no problem finding people willing to act for you. There may be a bigger problem in finding someone who has the appropriate qualities available at a price you can afford. As with other growth industries, there appear to be some people about who learned their trade selling snake oil. What are the characteristics of a good consultant? We offer the following criteria as a basis.

Educational background

This seems obvious, but some services are currently being offered by people with very limited educational experience. There is something to be said for a consultant who knows what schools are like and has experienced the kinds of challenges which face teachers daily. (You don't have to be a chicken to tell a good egg from a bad one, but neither would you presume to tell a hen how to lay them.)

Experience in the INSET field

Knowledge of INSET processes, contacts with others in the field, and hence an ability to suggest a range of options are of key importance.

Acceptability

You (and your staff) must be able to work with the consultant. This will depend not only upon personal qualities, but also upon 'street cred', which will derive from educational background and INSET experience.

Accessibility

This will depend on both geographical closeness and availability, i.e. will the consultant be able to come to the school, within reason, as and when required?

Consultancy experience

Everyone has to start some time and inevitably not all consultants can be very experienced (just as somebody has got to be a dentist's first patient). If the other criteria are met, the chances are that the consultant will do a good job, but obviously previous experience is a bonus.

Where to find a consultant

The director of your local teachers' centre is likely to match up with most of the above criteria and – perhaps even more importantly, because there is only one of him or her – will know of others who similarly qualify. These may be colleagues in colleges, polytechnics and other institutions of higher education with whom the teachers' centre personnel have been involved at courses, conferences or workshops. One additional advantage of using people from these institutions is that they are sufficiently distanced from the school and the LEA such that they can bring a neutral presence to the enterprise.

A member of the local advisory service or inspectorate could be an appropriate consultant: this will depend largely upon how the 'acceptability' criterion is met. Some teachers and some schools might have difficulty relating with an adviser or inspector, particularly when the topic under exploration is one that might be seen to overlap with the supervisory/evaluative functions of the adviser or inspector. Similarly, some inspectors find it difficult to shed the trappings of their status when entering into educational discussions with teachers.

An interesting use of experienced teachers has been reported (Beck and Kelly 1989). These were people engaged on a Diploma course on Management in Education at a Polytechnic and, as part of their programme, operated in teams as consultants in schools under the guidance and supervision of polytechnic staff. They were thus able to share their experience with other teacher colleagues and the consultancies were carried out within a supportive framework. Such mechanisms would seem to have much to commend them.

The role of consultant has been described as a 'licence to kill': this might be overly sceptical, but all involved should be aware of the implications and dangers. Many of these can be avoided if care is taken at the contract stage so that all parties are aware of their obligations as well as their rights. A consultant will be privy to a great deal of information about the school and the teachers within it: for any discussion, report or survey, it is important to establish how confidentiality will be maintained (if that is seen as desirable) and who will have access to any of the information and under what circumstances.

This is related to another issue: when does a consultancy end? This may not be as clear cut as it seems. If a consultant is recruited to help plan and run a single professional training day, the task may well not be complete at the end of that day. There may be (probably will be) aspects to be followed up, which may constitute an important element of any evaluation. Here it is worth while if all parties concerned remind themselves of the terms of the original contract, especially those aspects concerned with ownership and confidentiality.

What it will cost?

What will it cost? If you use someone from the advisory service or from a teachers' centre, they come (apparently) for free. There is, of course, a cost involved in that their time has to be accounted for. It is, of course, good management practice to be able to quantify the cost of such things, but as far as the school's capitation is concerned, there is no charge (at least not until LMS is in train).

Polytechnics, universities and colleges have usually delineated the fees applicable to such activities, and you might want to shop around. However, there may be little merit in going for cheapness for its own sake. An inexpensive consultancy is of little value if the quality is poor. A little intelligence-gathering could pay off here. If other schools have used people from an institution before, you should be able to get some impression from them – favourable or otherwise. See if you can gain access to any INSET information network. Again, someone from your local teachers' centre should be able to help you.

Individual, private consultants are becoming more numerous. Wherever possible you should take advice from a trusted colleague, preferably someone who knows the person and the quality of the consultant's work. In a world in which teachers have come to take for granted that such help, advice, knowledge and skills are available at no cost, it may come as a shock when the level of fees emerges. A daily rate of the order of £250–300 is the kind of 'ball-park' figure to have in mind, and your budget procedure for your professional training day should be planned accordingly. Good consultants rarely come cheaply, and you tend to get what you pay for. But then, 'if you think education is expensive, you should try ignorance'.

References

Abbot, R., Birchenough, M. and Steadman, S. (1988a) *GRIDS Primary School Handbook*, second edition, London: Longman (for SCDC).

Abbot, R., Birchenough, M. and Steadman, S. (1988b) *GRIDS Secondary School Handbook*, second edition, London: Longman (for SCDC).

Altrichter, H. (1986) 'The Austrian INSET Project', *British Journal of In-Service Education*, 13, 1: 170–7.

Beck, T. and Kelly, M. (1989) 'Using consultancy to help train managers in education', *British Journal of In-Service Education*, 15, 1: 19–24.

CIPFA (1988) *Local Management in Schools – A Practical Guide*, London: CIPFA, The Local Management in Schools Initiative.

DES (1988) *Education Reform Act: Local Management of Schools*, Circular 7/88, London: HMSO.

DES (1989) *Local Education Authority Training Grants Scheme: Financial Year 1990–91*, Circular 20/89, London: HMSO.

Eason, P. (1985) *Making School-centred INSET Work*, London: Open University/Croom Helm.

Easterby-Smith, M. (1986) *Evaluation of Management Education: Training and Development*, Aldershot: Gower.

Further Education Unit (1987) *Planning Staff Development: A Guide for Managers*, London: FEU.

Gough, R.G. (1976) 'The colleges of education and support for curriculum planning', *British Journal of In-Service Education*, 3, 1: 47–9.

Gough, R.G. (1985) 'Staff development – as part of the continuing education of teachers', *British Journal of In-Service Education*, 12, 1: 35–40.

Gough, R.G. and McGhee, J. (1980) *Curriculum Planning*, London: Schools Council.

Industrial Society (1982) *Effective Meetings*, London: Industrial Society Press.
Joyce, B. and Showers, B. (1981) 'Transfer of training', *Journal of Education*, 163, Spring.
LEAP (1990) *Local Education Authorities Project*, London: BBC/OU.
McMahon, A., Bolam, R. and Holly, P. (1984) 'Guidelines for Review and Internal Development of Schools (GRIDS), London: Schools Council Programme 1: Purpose and Planning in Schools.
Meetings, Bloody Meetings (1981) Video Arts, Dumbarton House, 68 Oxford Street, London WCIN 91A.
More Bloody Meetings (1984) Video Arts, Dumbarton House, 68 Oxford Street, London WCIN 91A.
National Curriculum Council (1989a) *The National Curriculum Information Pack No. 1*, London: National Curriculum Council.
National Curriculum Council (1989b) *Developing INSET Activities*, London: National Curriculum Council.
Nicholson, A., Joyce, B., Parker, D., and Waterman, F. (1976) *The Literature on In-Service Teacher Education: An Analytic Review*, Palo Alto, Calif: Stanford Center for Reseach and Development in Teaching.
Nuttall, D.L., McCormick, R., Turner, G., Holly, L., James, M., West, A. and Clift, P.S. (1987) *Studies in School Self Evaluation*, Lewes: Falmer Press.
Open University (1985) *Making School-centred INSET Work*, P536, Milton Keynes: Open University.
O'Sullivan, F., Jones, K., and Reid, K. (1988) *Staff Development in Secondary Schools*, London: Hodder & Stoughton.
Parlett, M. and Hamilton, D. (1972) *Evaluation as Illumination*, Centre for Research in the Educational Sciences, University of Edinburgh.
Posch, P. (1985) *University Support for Independent Learning*, Research Institute for Higher Education, Hiroshima University.
Schools Council (1978) 'Integration' 'Mixed Ability Teaching' (Materials for Curriculum Planning Unit).
Skilbeck, M. (1976) 'School-based Curriculum Development', in *Supporting Curriculum Development*, Open University Course E 203, Educational Studies, Curriculum Design and Development, Milton Keynes: Open University.
Stufflebeam, D.L., Foley, W.J., Gephart, W.J., Guba Egar, G., Hammond, R.I., Merriman, H.O. and Prows, M.M. (1971) *Educational Evaluation and Decision Making*, F.E. Peacock for Phi Delta Kappan, Itasca, Illinois.
Suffolk Education Department (1985) *Those Having Torches . . . Teacher Appraisal – A Study*, Ipswich: Suffolk Education Department.
Suffolk Education Department (1987) *In the Light of Torches*, London: The Industrial Society for Suffolk Education Department.
Thornbury, R. (Ed.) (1972) *Teacher Centres*, London: Darton, Longman & Todd.